FREEDOM, JUSTICE AND THE STATE

Ronald H. Nash
Western Kentucky University

University Press
of America™

Library of Congress Catalog Card Number: 80-8145

TO

MY BROTHER, GERALD

ACKNOWLEDGMENT

Grateful acknowledgment is made to the publishers of quoted material for permission to reprint from their sources. Full credit is given in the notes at the end of the book. In addition, special acknowledgement is made to the following publishers for their permission to quote:

From Capitalism and Freedom by Milton Friedman by permission of the University of Chicago Press. Copyright 1962.

From Capitalism and the Historians, edited by Friedrich A. Hayek by permission of The University of Chicago Press. Copyright 1954.

From Individualism and Economic Order by Friedrich A. Hayek by permission of The University of Chicago Press. Copyright 1948.

From Law, Legislation and Liberty, Vol. II: The Mirage of Social Justice by Friedrich A. Hayek by permission of The University of Chicago Press. Copyright 1976.

From Law, Legislation and Liberty, Vol. III: The Political Order of a Free People by Friedrich A. Hayek by permission of The University of Chicago Press. Copyright 1979.

From Natural Right and History by Leo Strauss by permission of The University of Chicago Press. Copyright 1953.

From Obscenity and Public Morality by Harry M. Clor by permission of The University of Chicago Press. Copyright 1969.

From Ethics, "Liberty Without Fraternity," by B.J. Diggs (Volume 87, January 1977) by permission of The University of Chicago Press.

From Ethics, "Welfare and Freedom," by Norman E. Bowie (Volume 89, April 1979) by permission of The University of Chicago Press.

From Monthly Review, "Socialism and Communism as Ideals, " by Paul Sweezy. Copyright © 1963 by

PREFACE

Any reflection about the nature of the good society must consider the many questions that can be raised about freedom, justice, and the State--perhaps the three major concepts of social philosophy. Many who today pretend to speak to issues of social concern appear quite uninformed about these basic notions. What do the terms "freedom" and "justice" mean? What is the State? Is the existence of the State justified? What are the proper limits of the power of the State? What about the intervention of the State in economic matters that gives rise to the disputes between advocates of capitalism, socialism, and the welfare state? These are some of the broader questions to be addressed in this book.

A prominent feature of almost all contemporary discussions of freedom and justice is the attempt to tie these concepts in some way to the institution of the State. It is widely assumed that freedom and justice require the support of a strong paternalistic and constantly intervening State. This assumption has become increasingly suspect as growing numbers of people come to believe that the State has grown too large for their good. Many Americans are beginning to doubt that government is the cure for their social problems; they are beginning to think it is their major cause.

Three major objectives of this book can be identified. Its first is to offer analyses of the three concepts named in its title. Chapter One attempts to answer the question, "What is the State?" Justice and freedom are analyzed in Chapters Two and Three.

Our second objective is to examine the commonly held assumption that the demands of freedom and justice support the contemporary aggrandizement of the State. The book examines and evaluates two radically different approaches to freedom and justice that presently compete for dominance. I call them the statist and anti-statist paths to freedom and justice. The two positions are described in Chapter One. Their implications for freedom and justice are discussed and appraised in Chapters Two and Three.

Our final purpose is the consideration of two vital areas of individual and social life, morality and economics, where questions about the practical applications of freedom and justice can become especially vexing. Chapter Four, "Freedom, Morality and the Law" begins with an investigation of the relationship between freedom and virtue. It moves to a consideration of the question, under what conditions do the moral concerns of society justify the enforcement of morality? The chapter explores the various liberty-limiting principles used to justify society's interference with individual freedom. Chapter Five, the first of two dealing with the economic issues, distinguishes three basic economic systems (capitalism, socialism, and interventionism). Socialism and interventionism are statist while capitalism, properly understood, is anti-statist. The chapter examines the importance and nature of economic freedom and its place in a market economy. It proceeds to an evaluation of the two dominant forms of economic statism, socialism and the mixed economy. The last chapter, "Reason, Morality, and the Market," lists and evaluates the major objections to a free market economy, objections used to justify statist intervention with the economy.

In order to distinguish between the radically different classical and contemporary versions of political liberalism, I adopted the convention of capitalizing Liberalism whenever I refer to the contemporary movement. Moreover, because of its prominence in my argument and because of the

view I hold, I have also followed the convention
of capitalizing the noun, "State." Naturally,
some of the sources I quote do not follow these
conventions.

A number of organizations and individuals
have contributed to the writing of this book. The
work began in 1969 with research supported by a
fellowship from the National Endowment for the
Humanities. Western Kentucky University helped in
many ways including several leaves for research
and writing. Carol Horne typed the final copy.
My secretary, Brenda Lane, and her corps of student assistants worked on earlier drafts. Steve
Baker, my graduate assistant in 1979-80, was a
great help in providing transcriptions from oral
presentations. Several friends and colleagues
read early drafts and provided valuable sugges-
tions. They include: Rob Johnston, Bill Lane,
Larry Mayhew, Bob Roberts, Ted Schoen, Jim
Spiceland, and Arvin Vos. Special thanks must go
to Charles Van Eaton of Hillsdale College who will
recognize some of his own ideas scattered throughout the work. Bill Buckley's advice at a difficult point in the argument helped me handle an
especially vexing problem.

Some of this material has been presented as
lectures at a number of colleges including
Wheaton College, Seattle-Pacific University,
Houghton College, Asbury Theological Seminary,
Covenant College, and Hillsdale College. The lecture at Hillsdale is copyrighted by its Center for
Constructive Alternatives and I appreciate permission to include portions of it at various
points throughout the book. I also appreciate
permission from the editors of The Intercollegiate
Review and Christianity Today to include material
from some of my articles previously published in
their journals. The articles are cited in the
bibliography.

The work could never have been completed
without the understanding and support of my wife,
Betty Jane, and my children, Jeff and Jennifer.

TABLE OF CONTENTS

CHAPTER ONE

STATISM AND THE STATE

What is the State? Those who seek to profit from the power of the State have done a good job of passing it off as a benevolent friend ready to help in every time of need. One of their more successful moves has been to blur the distinction between the State and society. The State, they affirm, is simply an extension of our own corporate desires. Great harm has resulted from the myth that the State is simply a projection of "us," that it is in some sense the totality of the people. Once a people falls under the spell that "We are the State," they can easily be manipulated to accept anything the State does on the grounds that they are only doing it to themselves.

The State is the group of individuals which actually runs a nation, makes its laws, issues its commands, punishes those regarded in violation of the rules, and acquires the money required to run the machinery of the State.

> The state is not co-extensive with the totality of that which it governs; it is a definite group of men, distinct and separate from other men, a group of men possessing the monopoly of legal coercive force. And it remains thus set off, separate, whether it governs with or without the consent of the governed, with or without their participation in the choice of the governors. Even in a democratic polity, the state is not 'we,' identical with all the people, as is so often claimed; it is 'they,' those who hold state power.[1]

A State then is not just an organized group of people located within some specified territorial boundary. Always, within each of these geographical groupings, the actual orders are issued by a much smaller group that makes the laws and forces the others to obey. The group that rules may be one or many. Its power will be sustained and enhanced by the support of a group of loyal followers; but the State itself is identical with the person or group that holds the power.[2]

Many social philosophers have insisted that the State be distinguished from society. Felix Morley, a strong advocate of the distinction, has suggested that society is marked by the voluntary character of its associations whereas the State is always characterized by its use of force, by its unwillingness to depend upon the voluntary support of the people. Compulsion is not an essential feature of the companionship found in a society. For Morley, societies are not only voluntary association; they also share "a common interest, a common objective, [and] to some extent a common faith...."[3] Morley argues that the associations that characterize the State are not voluntary. "The State, in short, subjects people: whereas Society associates them voluntarily."[4] Whereas "society" means "every form of voluntary association directed to the self-defined benefit of individuals," the State is "the dominant organization which has gradually acquired the power to dictate both to individuals and to social groupings under its sovereignty...."[5]

Robert A. Nisbet concurs in locating the essential difference between society and State in the State's use of force and coercion. He writes, "Unlike the State which rests upon force the social groups in society rest upon the reciprocal principle of friendship.... The principle of mutual responsibility is the very structure of" societal relationships.[6] The basic difference between a society and the State then is the indispensible place of force and power in the latter. The State always supports its claim to the obedience of its followers through the use of force. The force may be blatant as in the case of armies, prisons or firing squads; or it may be applied more subtly in the form of threats. But wherever the State exists, one will necessarily find coercion.[7]

THE EXALTATION OF THE STATE

Contemporary civilization is threatened by the aggrandizement of the State, by what José Ortega y Gasset calls "the absorption of all spontaneous social effort by the State."[8] Albert Jay Nock warned that "If we look beneath the surface of our public affairs, we can discern one fundamental fact, namely: a great redistribution of power between society and the State."[9] Felix Morley observed that "Man has for centuries fulfilled his destiny within the framework of Society. But there are many indications that he is now exchanging membership in Society for servitude to the State."[10] The State justifies its confiscation of power from society on the ground that society has failed to exert enough power to meet the emergencies that have confronted it. Our name for this exaltation of the State is "statism."

"Statism" and "anti-statism" are not easy terms to define. Neither is a simple or fixed position. Each term covers a multitude of sins. One approach to clarifying the meaning of the two words is to imagine a continuum with statism on one end and anti-statism on the other.[11]

ANTI-STATISM   STATISM

0   100
_____

Anarchism   Totalitar-
(total re-   the   the   ianism
pudiation   minimal   maximal
of the   State   State
State)

3

The marks of more radical forms of statism are easy to recognize. Radical statists tend to view the State as an end in itself rather than as a means to achieving the ends of individual human beings. Frequently, extreme statists hypostatize what is nothing more than a set of relationships among many individual human beings into an existing being or organism that has its own life, moral duties, and rights. In Rousseau's statism, the function of the State

> is to effectuate the independence of the individual from society by securing the individual's dependence upon itself. The State is the means by which the individual can be freed of the restrictive tyrannies that compose society.... What Rousseau calls freedom is at bottom no more than the freedom to do what the State in its omniscience determines. Freedom for Rousseau is the synchronization of all social existence to the will of the State, the replacement of cultural diversity by a mechanical equalitarianism.[12]

Rousseau's enhancement of the State held obvious implications for his view of human freedom. As Nisbet explains, Rousseau believed that

> True freedom consists in the willing subordination of the individual to the whole of the State. If this is not forthcoming, compulsion is necessary; but this merely means that the individual 'will be forced to be free.'[13]

Radical statism also appears frequently to deify the State. Hegel went so far as to speak of the State as God's Spirit in the world. In its Fascist forms, statism asserts that the individual is nothing, while the State is everything. Mussolini, for example, wrote that Fascism

> is for the individual in so far as he coincides with the State, which is the conscience

4

and universal will of man in his historical
existence.... Fascism reaffirms the State as
the true reality of the individual.

The only liberty Mussolini favored was the freedom
of the individual to do what the State commanded.
In his chilling words, "Therefore, for the Fascist, everything is in the State, and nothing
human or spiritual exists, much less has value,
outside the State."[14]

STATISM AND SOCIAL ENGINEERING

Social engineering is a corollary of statism.
Social engineering (or its equivalent, political
rationalism) is the belief that the best social
order is a product of purposeful and deliberate
human design rather than the result of spontaneous
development.[15] The social engineer believes that
man has both the knowledge and the power to create
a better social order through the State. The
rationalist is never satisfied with any feature of
society that comes about automatically, as the
result of some mechanical[16] process like the market. Human planning and centralized control could
have always produced something better, he thinks.
He is out to redesign society according to his
blueprint, and the easiest way to accomplish his
end is to use the State. Social engineering would
be impossible apart from statism.

Social engineering threatens individual human
freedom and the voluntary communities that play
such an important role in the development of individual persons. Political rationalism is objectionable on the ground that it misconceives the
role of human reason with regard to society in at
least three ways. First, political rationalism
misunderstands the place that human reason has
played in the past development of civilization.
The rationalist errs in thinking that civilization
has developed as a result of conscious, deliberate
planning. On the contrary, society has grown to a

great extent because of the development of tools and institutions, such as money and the market, which men use without total comprehension. Civilization is not a result of rational manipulation and planning, but of trial and error. Human society exhibits an order that does not result from conscious human planning. In the words of Adam Ferguson, the 18th century Scottish philosopher, such an order is "the result of human action, but not the execution of any human design."[17] Friedrich Hayek expresses much the same view when he writes,

> By tracing the combined effects of individual actions, we discover that many of the institutions on which human achievements rest have arisen and are functioning without a designing and directing mind...and that the spontaneous collaboration of free men often creates things which are greater than their individual minds can ever fully comprehend.[18]

Voluntary and spontaneous cooperation can accomplish much more than the coercive manipulation of society by idealistic zealots.

One obvious example of such an order-producing mechanism is the market. Each participant in the market process receives signs or indicators of what needs other people want satisfied at a particular time and for a particular price. Without these indicators, the actor in the market would never know which needs of other people he should aim to satisfy. The prices at which goods and services are selling is one such indicator which supplies important information telling each person in the market how best to direct his own efforts. Without the market mechanism, there would be no way to know the needs and wants of more than a few people. The success of some in the market provides indicators that point to directions others should take if they desire similar success. Of course, when that part of the market becomes too crowded, the signals will change and the wise actor will be ready to switch his activity in accordance with the new signals. This informational function of the market is negated more or less by governmental intervention with the market process. Factors such as prices and interest rates which might tell the wary agent something in an unhampered market become, following the manipulations of the interventionist, distorted and misleading signals that can provide no clear direction. Governmental intervention that effectively nullified the signals from this mechanical process contributed to every economic crisis in America's history.[19]

The political rationalist's second error is overestimating the power and scope of human knowledge in solving social problems. The social engineer exaggerates the power of human reason to achieve genuine improvements in society. The rationalist assumes that human reason is sufficient, in spite of the complicated relationships that exist among the infinite number of variables, to identify social programs that will improve society as a whole. It should be obvious that the social sciences cannot attain the same degree of specificity and preciseness in their predictions and explanations as the natural sciences. But the social engineer refuses to take account of this fact. His efforts to predict and control what society will do only compounds the problems of society. This is one important reason why so many programs proposed as solutions for social ills end up creating even greater problems.

Thirdly, the social engineer also ignores the complexities of the social units (by which I mean the individual human beings) he seeks to manipulate. He forgets that men do more than act; they also react when they are pushed or pulled; and their reactions are often surprisingly unpredictable. The social engineer treats men as faceless and windowless monads whom he thinks he can shuffle like pieces on a game board or like children on a school bus.[20] He thinks that change A will produce effect B, and that C will cause D, and

that E will cause F, all predictable by him and
his cohorts. The rationalist believes he has several separate elements, each one of which is an
improvement on a prior situation, and thinks he
can build a better society simply by joining these
elements together. What he forgets, given the
chemistry of human action and reaction, is that
the forcing of the various relations together may
produce an explosion. But he also has an answer
for that. Unleash the power of the State and
force the people to accept his will. After all,
he knows what is best for them; he knows what they
really want.

Social engineering should be abandoned,
therefore, because it is blind to the extremely
restricted role that reason has played in the past
history of civilization, because it overlooks the
obvious limitations of human knowledge in the
social sciences, and because it ignores the unpre-
dictability and complexity of the individual human
beings it attempts to control. The serious errors
within the theory that underlies social engineering, the devastating effect of many of its programs on American society, and its influence on
the American State provide clues for the growing
influence of anti-statism in America.

ANTI-STATISM

It is important to distinguish two quite different types of anti-statism. (1) Radical anti-
statism is opposed to any and every State; it
attacks the State per se. Many anti-statists in
this first sense openly embrace or at least look
longingly on anarchism. Even when a radical anti-
statist concludes that he cannot accept anarchism,
he accepts the legitimacy of a minimal or limited
State begrudgingly.

(2) Moderate anti-statism is not opposed to
the State per se; its attacks are directed against
a particular kind of State. Few writers have
articulated this position more clearly than Robert

Nisbet. Basic to Nisbet's position is the contrast he draws between two kinds of State: the
society-denying State and the society-affirming
State. Nisbet believes that the kind of State
that threatens society

> seeks always to extend its administrative
> powers and functions into all realms of soci-
> ety, always seeking a higher degree of cen-
> tralization in the conduct of its operations,
> always tending toward a wider measure of
> politicization of social, economic, and cul-
> tural life. It does not do this in the name
> of power but of freedom--freedom from want,
> insecurity, and minority tyranny. It parades
> the symbols of progress, people, justice,
> welfare, and devotion to the common man....
> It builds up a sense of the absolute identity
> of State and Society--nothing outside the
> State, everything in the State.[21]

Nisbet continues:

> Increasingly, in this type of State, the
> basic needs for education, recreation, wel-
> fare, economic production, distribution, and
> consumption, health, spiritual and physical,
> and all other services of society are made
> aspects of the administrative structure of
> political government.[22]

Nisbet thinks it is basically irrelevant whether
such a State masquerades as democratic or humanitarian; every contemporary totalitarianism has
claimed to be such. "The impersonal despotism of
virture...is not the less despotic because it is
virtuous."[23]

Nisbet correctly notes that Totalitarianism
is the ultimate enemy

> of those social relationships within which
> individuality develops. It is not the exter-
> mination of individuals that is ultimately
> desired by totalitarian rulers, for

9

individuals in the largest number are needed
by the new order. What is desired is the
extermination of those social relationships
which, by their autonomous existence, must
always constitute a barrier to the achievement of the absolute political community.[24]

Totalitarian rulers know only too well how powerless the individual is apart from the societies
that nourish and sustain him.

The prime object of totalitarian government
thus becomes the incessant destruction of all
evidences of spontaneous, autonomous association. For, with this social atomization,
must go also a diminution of intensity and a
final flickering out of political values that
interpose themselves between freedom and
despotism.[25]

The society-denying State, then, seeks to consoli-
date its power over the individual, not by
directly threatening the individual, but by seeking

to destroy or diminish the reality of the
smaller areas of society, to abolish or
restrict the range of cultural alternatives
offered individuals by economic endeavor,
religion, and kinship....[26]

This in turn will lead to totalitarianism because
it will eventually weaken the individual's resistance to tyranny.

In its negative aspects totalitarianism is
thus a ceaseless process of cultural nihilism.
How else can the individual be separated from
the traditions and values which, if allowed
to remain intact, would remind him constantly
of his cultural past? A sense of the past is
far more basic to the maintenance of freedom
than hope for the future. The former is con-
crete and real; the latter is necessarily
amorphous and more easily guided by those who

10

can manipulate human actions and beliefs.
Hence the relentless techniques for abolish-
ing the social allegiances within which the
individual memory is given strength and power
of resistance.[27]

Social philosophers like Nisbet are moderate
anti-statists in the sense that they oppose only
those States that seek, consciously or uncon-
sciously, to attack or undermine the voluntary
communal dimensions of the individual's life.
Nisbet is supportive of States that recognize the
point at which their power is limited by the
social sphere. This second type of State, the
society-affirming State,

> seeks, without sacrificing its legitimate
> sovereignty grounded in the will of the peo-
> ple, to maintain a pluralism of functions and
> loyalties in the lives of its people. It is
> a State that knows that the political absorp-
> tion of the institutional functions of an
> association, be it family, local community,
> or trade union, must soon be followed by the
> loss or weakening of psychological devotions
> to the association. It is a State that seeks
> to diversify and decentralize its own admini-
> strative operations and to relate these as
> closely as possible to the forms of sponta-
> neous association which are the outgrowth of
> human needs and desires and which have rele-
> vance to the economic, educational, and reli-
> gious ends of a culture.[28]

The first kind of State, the society-denying
State, either negates society or seeks to absorb
society into its own orb. "However broad its base
in the electorate and however nobly inspired its
rulers," Nisbet warns, such a State "must always
border upon despotism."[29] Because the society-
affirming State, is pluralistic, not monolithic,

> its power will be limited by associations
> whose plurality of claims upon their members

11

is the measure of their members' freedom from
any monopoly of power in society.[30]

Nisbet, then, typifies those moderate anti-
statists who stop short of opposing the very
institution of the State. Their attacks are
reserved for those States that seek to usurp the
functions of voluntary human associations.

STATISM AND THE MODERN LIBERAL

It is difficult to find any contemporary
anti-statist who does not regard his condemnation
of statism as an indictment of contemporary political Liberalism. All seem agreed that the kind of
political Liberalism advocated by the Kennedy
brothers, George McGovern, John Kenneth Galbraith,
Walter Mondale, and the late Hubert Humphrey is a
species of statism. M. Stanton Evans, for example, claims that the contemporary Liberal is

> profoundly distrustful of individual freedom
> and of arrangements arrived at through volun-
> tary action. [The Liberal] believes that pat-
> terns of human behavior under such arrange-
> ments are usually wrong, harmful, stupid, or
> malicious, and that they should be prevented
> by the constant and pervasive attention of
> the government.
> This fact is obvious enough to anyone who
> reflects on the general drift of American
> politics. It is difficult to think of a sin-
> gle problem area in our economic life to
> which the liberal response is not a demand
> for government intervention. If there be
> inflation, the liberal calls for wage and
> price controls. If we confront an energy
> crisis, the obvious answer is to regulate the
> relevant industries. If consumers want bet-
> ter products, establish a consumer czar with
> sweeping regulatory powers. If urban prob-
> lems plague us, we need bigger and better
> Federal subsidies. Whatever the trouble,
> real or imagined, the reflexive liberal

12

answer is to put more power in the hands of
government.[31]

Evans believes the political record of the past
several decades supports his contention that the
views he has described faithfully represent contemporary American Liberalism. Evans continues:

> The writings of the most noted and respected
> liberal spokesmen reveal a profound distrust
> of unhindered individual action, and yield
> repeated statements that a system of volun-
> tary exchange is destructive, both socially
> and economically. On countless occasions the
> liberal sages have stressed the need to put
> the values of the group above the freedom of
> the person.[32]

Public pronouncements of the Liberal organization, Americans for Democratic Action, provide
one support for Evans' contention. Its 1964 plat-
form, for example, affirmed that

> The blind forces of the market place cannot
> be depended upon either to achieve full
> employment and vigorous economic growth or to
> direct economic resources in accordance with
> national priorities. For these purposes we
> need democratic national economic planning to
> evaluate our resources and our needs and to
> develop an order of priorities for the appli-
> cation of resources to our needs....[33]

The ADA's call for a national planning agency
echoed Walter Reuther's 1963 plea for "some
mechanism to bring a rational sense of direction
into private decisions...only a national planning
agency can provide this direction."[34] Further
evidence of the extent to which Liberalism and
statism overlap is available in Harry Girvetz's
apology for Liberalism, The Evolution of Liberalism. According to Girvetz, the contemporary
political Liberal repudiates the classical liberalism of the nineteenth century because it was
insufficiently statist.[35] In the words of

13

Girvetz,

> Contemporary Liberalism differs markedly from
> the classical liberalism of the eighteenth
> and nineteenth centuries. To define this
> difference is to treat of the central social
> problem of our day: the degree to which we
> shall have collective control of individual
> behavior--the degree, that is, to which indi-
> vidual interests shall be subordinated to
> social purposes.[36]

There must be no mistake about the nature of the
collective control about which Girvetz writes so
enthusiastically. He means that the power of the
State should be used in order to subordinate individual interests to the concerns of some collective whole. The Liberalism represented by Girvetz
clearly falls into the kind of statism that seeks
to negate or absorb society. It is difficult to
imagine any reflective person familiar with the
recent national scene in America who would doubt
the claim that Liberalism is a form of statism.
Taken by itself, this judgment need not be pejora-
tive. In fact, most Liberals are proud of the
fact.

Statism attracts converts for a variety of
reasons. Some men simply lust for power and statism provides the quickest and most convenient
route to the attainment of power. But many have
turned to statism on allegedly humanitarian
grounds. Contemporary political Liberalism is
simply the most influential manifestation of the
humanitarian form of statism in this century. The
Liberal approach to freedom and justice is a logical extension of the primacy it gives the State.
The contemporary Liberal statist contends that the
freedom of many Americans is threatened because of
the State's inability or refusal to become more
active. Moreover, the Liberal claims, many people
need deliverance from the debilitating effects of
poverty, ignorance, and the corrupting influence
of big business. Only a powerful (and hopefully
benevolent) State can provide this needed

14

protection and can furnish a framework within which "genuine freedom" can thrive. As some Liberal writers see it, true freedom involves much more than being free from constraints and coercion. True freedom also requires the ability or the power to do or to be certain things. And so, the State must take action in order to enhance positive freedom. Millions of Americans are supposed to be living in literal bondage, not because America is a police state or because assorted coercive powers restrain them in some way, but simply because there are many things they are powerless to do or have. For anyone who believes this, it is a short step to the conclusion that the State must step in and help these people, because only then can they become truly free.

A similar bias in favor of the State infuses much Liberal thinking about justice. Once "justice" is understood in its distributive sense, as related to the way goods and burdens are distributed within a society, the entrance of the State into such considerations is inevitable. Clearly, statism is a powerful force in much current U. S. political thought. And one of its more important justifications is the claim that the demands of freedom and justice naturally support and, indeed require statist action. In his desire to achieve his social goals by the quickest possible means, the contemporary Liberal concentrates as much power as possible in the one institution able to override all obstacles, the State. As one Liberal member of Congress admitted several years ago, Liberals believe "in using the full force of government for the advancement" of their social goals.[37] Given the recent dominance of Liberalism in the political life of America, and given its commitment to statist solutions to social and political problems, it is only natural that freedom and justice have come to be viewed as inseparable from statist action. However the Liberal construes the problems of his nation, however compassionate and altruistic his professed goals, he believes those objectives can only be attained through the instrument of statist power.

15

Critics of Liberalism argue that the position is destructive of freedom and justice. One such opponent, the respected German economist, Wilhelm Röpke, warned that the greatest threat to a free society

> is the state itself.... The state and the concentration of its power...have become a cancerous growth gnawing at the freedom and order of society and economy.[38]

Nothing, the opponents of Liberalism maintain, threatens the existence of freedom and justice more than the contemporary rush toward statism.

THE STATIST ESTABLISHMENT

The late Frank Meyer contended that the contemporary State in America is controlled by a Liberal establishment composed of all those individuals and special interest groups who see their well-being dependent upon the continued favors of the State. Once the State achieves the power it needs to become the Liberal's purveyor of social justice, it is also powerful enough to become the dispenser of special privilege. As men seek hedges against the uncertainties and insecurities of life by establishing advantages over their competitors, they find it convenient to use the Liberal's all-powerful State to gain an edge. Meyer perceived the bureaucratic elite in America as

> a composite of several groups with different functional positions and some different parochial interest, but with an essential unity of ideological outlook and underlying interest that becomes greater year by year.[39]

Meyer viewed the bureaucracy as a four-headed beast that he called the Quadripartite Bureaucracy because it manifests itself in four different ways: (1) the governmental bureaucracy; (2) the salaried managers who control both the trade unions and the big corporations; (3) the mass-

16

communications bureaucracy; and (4) the academic
bureaucracy. In other words, the power of Leviathan extends not only to the massive governmental
bureaucracy but also to big labor and big business, to the media, and to education. The rise of
this Quadripartite Bureaucracy is a fairly recent
phenomenon, since fifty years ago none of these
bureaucracies existed or at least had the power
they presently have.

The liberal-collectivist bureaucratic elite
has little direct resemblance to the conscious unity of, say, a Communist Party. It
is quadripartite, not unified. Its four parts
(governmental, corporate-trade union, mass
communications, and academic) are often more
conscious of their differences and rivalries
than of their common aims. But the identity
of their underlying ideology impels them to
a common front whenever and wherever basic
issues are raised that would tend towards the
restoration of the conditions of freedom.
When they struggle among themselves, it is to
gain some particular advantage for one group
or another within the general bureaucratic
system. Any radical challenge to the basic
concepts upon which the power of the state is
based, they unite instinctively to oppose
with all the resources of their immense power.
The state is their hope and their future.
Without it their very function would cease to
be bureaucrats engineering their segment of
the grand design to reconstruct mankind.[40]

Each segment of the bureaucracy perceives its
present power as derived from the State; each
cooperates with the State in seeking special priv-
ileges and greater power. The Liberal cause has
been helped to no small extent through a remarkable slight of hand in which many have been led to
believe that the contemporary Liberal is actually
a courageous rebel doing battle with an essentially conservative establishment. Nothing could be
further from the truth. According to Meyer, the
American Establishment is a Liberal establishment

17

composed of those individuals and special interest groups who see their well-being as dependent upon the continued favors of the State. Liberals are not enemies of the establishment; they _are_ the establishment.

THE STATIST TRANSFORMATION OF THE STATE

Surely, it would seem, wise men would anticipate the inveterate tendency to enhance the power of the State, and find ways to limit the growth of its power. In fact, safeguards of this kind were utilized by the American Founding Fathers. But statists refuse to accept limits on the power of the State. Time after time, the very instruments designed to check statist power have been used as justifications for expanding the power of the State. In a perceptive discussion of how the State transcends its limits, Murray Rothbard draws attention to the many ways in which

> the State, using its intellectual allies, has been able to transform these limiting concepts into intellectual rubber stamps of legitimacy and virtue to attach to its decrees and actions.[41]

Originally, the concept of divine sovereignty was designed as one such limitation. Kings were to rule as themselves subject to the law of God. However, Rothbard notes,

> the kings turned the concept of divine sovereignty into a rubber stamp of divine approval for any of the kings' actions. The concept of parliamentary democracy began as a popular check upon absolute monarchial rule; it ended with parliament being the essential part of the state and its every act totally sovereign.[42]

Many of the original checks built into the United States Constitution have been used to justify expansions of statist power. While the

18

concept of judicial review was originally a check
against expansionist tendencies on the part of the
executive or legislative branches of government,
it has become a tool by which, in effect, new laws
are introduced through judicial "interpretation."
As Rothbard notes,

> the State has...largely transformed judicial
> review itself from a limiting device to yet
> another instrument for furnishing ideological
> legitimacy to the government's actions. For
> if a judicial decree of "unconstitutional"
> is a mighty check to government power, an
> implicit or explicit verdict of "constitu-
> tional" is a mighty weapon for fostering pub-
> lic acceptance of ever-greater government
> power.[43]

One recent example of how judicial "interpretation" has the effect of creating new law is the
Supreme Court's decision regarding abortion on
demand. Judicial review is but one example of how
the American system of constitutional checks upon
the power of the State has been dismantled.[44]

The American Founding Fathers were realists
when it came to human nature. They knew better
than to think that any group of men could be
trusted with unchecked power. Because of this
conviction, they created a complicated and cumbersome system of government in which various checks
and balances served to make the attainment of
absolute power by any one man or group extremely
difficult, if not impossible. But a complicated
and decentralized political system that acts as a
restraint to totalitarianism is also an obstacle
to the quick realization of the statist's dreams.
And so, one by one, statists in America have been
able, with remarkable success, to dismantle the
system given by the Founding Fathers.

ANARCHISM

Anarchism is the most extreme form of anti-

19

statism. For an anarchist, it is not enough just
to attack statism. He believes that the real
problem lies with the institution of the State
itself. A brief examination of anarchism can
serve as a helpful introduction to all the forms
of anti-statism that are suspicious of the State
per se.

Anarchism is the belief that social order can
be achieved and preserved, and social chaos
avoided, without resorting to the State. Anarchism challenges the very legitimacy of the State.
The anarchist armory contains a wide variety of
arguments against the State, only a few of which
will be noted here.[45]

One of the more persuasive anarchist arguments is its attack on the moral legitimacy of the
State. This proceeds in two ways. First of all,
anarchists denounce the State as immoral because
it violates human rights. Critics of the State
regard it "as the supreme, the eternal, the best
organized, aggressor against the persons and property of the mass of the public."[46] Because the
State always holds a monopoly on the use of coercive power within its boundaries, it possesses the
power to engage in actions which, if committed by
any private citizen or by a non-statist institution, would be deemed criminal. The State

> claims and exercises the monopoly of crime....
> It forbids private murder, but itself orga-
> nizes murder on a colossal scale. It pun-
> ishes private theft, but itself lays unscru-
> pulous hands on anything it wants, whether
> the property of citizen or of alien.[47]

John Hospers writes,

> Government is the most dangerous institution
> known to man. Throughout history it has vio-
> lated the rights of men more than any indi-
> vidual or group of individuals could do: it
> has killed people, enslaved them, sent them
> to forced labor and concentration camps, and

regularly robbed them of the fruits of their
expended labor.[48]

If every human being has the right to live his
life as he chooses so long as he does not violate
the rights of others to do the same, the existence
of an institution that forcibly violates that
right is wrong.

While there is much truth in the anarchist's
moral indictment of the State, the argument fails
to prove that the State is inherently immoral.
Even if every State that has ever existed misused
its powers and violated human rights, it would not
follow from this alone that the State is essentially wicked. The conclusion requires evidence
that the State necessarily violates human rights.
Unfortunately for the anarchist, the high degree
of probability that is the most that follows from
his study of the State's past record is not enough
to establish his case. If the anarchist argument
is to succeed, the immorality of the State can not
simply be an incidental though frequently recur-
ring feature. The criminal nature of the State
would need to be shown as a necessary and unavoidable feature of all States. But this is something
the anarchist cannot do.

The second anarchist attack argues that the
State is immoral because it is by its very nature,
a parasite upon society. This claim was developed
more than fifty years ago by a German sociologist,
Franz Oppenheimer, who drew attention to the two
mutually exclusive ways in which wealth can be
acquired.[49] The first method of acquiring wealth,
which Oppenheimer called "the economic means,"
requires that human beings first use their minds,
talents, and energy to produce some resource.
These people can then exchange what they have produced for products that others have brought into
existence. Oppenheimer claimed that this method
of producing goods and then exchanging them is the
natural means of acquiring wealth. Instead of
fighting over scarce resources which would result
in one man's acquiring a resource at the expense

21

of another, it is to men's advantage to transfer
products in the peaceful context of a free market
exchange. Not only does it work to each person's
mutual benefit, the peaceful and voluntary
exchanges of a free market tend to multiply the
resources.

The second way of acquiring wealth, called by
Oppenheimer "the political means," does not
require productivity and seldom allows peaceful
and voluntary exchanges. The acquisition of
wealth in this method takes place by force and
violence as one group of people confiscates (by
theft or exploitation) the wealth that others have
produced. The political means is parasitic; it
could never exist by itself. Because it does not
produce anything new, it can only function by
siphoning off that which others have produced to
a non-producing individual or group. Oppenheimer
defined the State as "the organization of the
political means." The State as such does not produce. While it may masquerade as the protector of
the producers, the elite that control the State
are in effect predators. Since the State does not
produce but preys upon those who do, the very survival of the State depends upon the continued
existence of a large class of producers. The most
effective class of predators will be small. The
survival of the State requires that the largest
segment of society continue to produce. But the
parasitic nature of statist activity helps destroy
the incentive of the producer to produce more than
he needs for himself. Frequently, the State loses
sight of how important it is to keep the size of
the producing class large. A too generous welfare
state, for example, might make it so attractive
for people not to produce that many would be
encouraged to stop producing and join the ranks of
the non-producers. While this might help the
predators win elections, it would prove suicidal
since the robbers would dissipate the resources
needed for their own subsistence.

Any adequate presentation of the anarchist
case requires two steps. First, the anarchist

must succeed in showing that the State is necessarily and unavoidably immoral or wrong. Even if
this first step is successful, the anarchist ought
to be able to show how an anarchist society could
provide for social order without resorting to the
machinery of the State. Contemporary anarchism is
usually presented in one of two forms: anarcho-
socialism and anarcho-capitalism. The writings of
socialistic anarchists are especially disappoint-
ing in this regard. They usually refuse to offer
any models of how their socialistic society can
attain order without reinstituting the coercion of
the State. The only reason given for their
silence is the disclaimer that they are not in the
business of predicting the future or preparing
blueprints for utopia.

Tibor Machan doubts that socialist forms of
anarchism are realistic. He points out, for
example, that

> leftist and Marxist-oriented anarchists advo-
> cate that all property be held communally or
> collectively but that no government should
> exist to keep people from running away with
> some of it! Anarchocommunism is, at best, a
> vision; it depends on the idea or faith that
> humanity will someday develop into a differ-
> ent species, one whose members will do every-
> thing "right," automatically, in an environ-
> ment of full abundance, with no scarcity. If
> that were possible then, indeed, the purpose
> of government and law could no longer make
> sense--there would certainly be no need to
> protect and preserve human rights and legal
> justice; it would happen anyway, automati-
> cally.[50]

Machan's suspicion concerning the anarcho-
socialist is justified. If it is a workable society for human beings that is being sought instead
of a pipedream about some new species supposedly
free from all human weaknesses, anarcho-socialism
should be ignored. Machan is correct in dispar-
aging Marxist anarchism as utopian, in the worst

sense of the word.

It is utopian in the sense that what it promises for some type of creatures is not something that can be held out to human beings with any expectation that the promise might be fulfilled. At any rate, there is no rational reason to anticipate the realization of Marxist communism while there are human beings who ought to find the best form of community life for themselves.[51]

Another influential form of anarchism, anarcho-capitalism, has attempted to provide models of how social order would be provided in a stateless society.[52] It is for this reason that anarcho-capitalism seems a more promising alternative. As anarchists like Murray Rothbard and David Friedman explain, the anarchist is not necessarily an apologist for social disorder; he does not repudiate the need for social order. However, the anarchist insists, the social institutions that make social order possible must be voluntary. In a sense, any voluntary, non-statist organization can be an example of an anarchistic group. The family, churches, clubs, and the myriad of other voluntary organizations in society all show the feasibility of anarchism on a small scale. According to the model of anarcho-capitalism, all of society's basic needs can and should be met by voluntary means, for example, by the replacement of public libraries with private renting libraries, or the formation of voluntary kibbutz that would provide health services, housing and education.

But here too the question of realism must be raised. The basic fault of the anarchist position is its unrealistic view of human nature. It is simply a half-truth, as Tuccille claims, that "the real enemy is not other people, but the state-- the violent and oppressive nature of government itself."[53] The enemy includes the State, no doubt. But, unfortunately, it also includes a number of other people. Embezzlers, perpetrators

24

of fraud, stick-up men, psychopathic killers, and potential rapists are not going to disappear when the State goes out of business. It is unlikely that the activities of people like these will decrease without adequate protection against their criminal aggression.

Can an anarchist society be protected from invasion by external enemies who would destroy any vestige of individual liberty? Unless a society can defend itself against the threat of invasion, it won't be free for very long. The comments of David Friedman suggest a semblance of realism still remains among a few anarchists. He asks if a society might be able to raise enough money to support a national defense agency through voluntary means without resorting to taxation. (The introduction of taxation would simply be a reintroduction of the State.) Friedman thinks it might be possible to provide national defense by voluntary contributions; but he's not sure. Neither am I. What, Friedman asks, would he do if he became convinced that national security required the forcible taking of money by taxation?

> In such a situation, I would not try to abolish that last vestige of government. I do not like paying taxes, but I would rather pay them to Washington than to Moscow--the rates are lower. I would still regard the government as a criminal organization, but one which was, by a freak of fate, temporarily useful. It would be like a gang of bandits who, while occasionally robbing the villages in their territory, served to keep off other and more rapacious gangs. I do not approve of any government, but I will tolerate one, so long as the only other choice is another, worse government.[54]

There is no need to elaborate on the obvious problems here. Since any anarchistic society in the real world must provide national defense and internal security in order to guarantee the survival of liberty, and since it is impossible to see how these defense forces could be maintained without forcing people to contribute to their costs, it seems unlikely that an anarchistic society can provide security without resorting to the coercive measures of a State. Perhaps the best analysis of the security problem as the achilles heel of anarchism has been provided by Robert Nozick in his Anarchy, State and Utopia. Nozick dismantles anarcho-capitalism by showing that it leads inevitably to a social order that resembles a minimal State. He does this by focusing on the kinds of private protection agencies that play such an important role in systems like that of Murray Rothbard. In the anarchist's state of nature, conflicts arising between persons require them to purchase aid and defense by hiring private security forces. The ensuing competition between private protection agencies would result in some being more successful than others. Less successful agencies would either disappear (go out of business) or merge into larger protection agencies that would soon assume the basic features of a minimal State. Nozick's argument points out the unavoidability of the State, even in allegedly anarchistic societies.[55]

The inadequacy of the Rothbard anarcho-capitalist model is apparent on other grounds as well. Rothbard acknowledges his fundamental commitment to human rights. Indeed, the basis for his opposition of the State is his belief that all States are immoral because they necessarily infringe upon fundamental natural rights. But it should be obvious that the natural rights of some human beings cannot be preserved in a society where protection against aggression must be purchased from private protection agencies. Ostensibly, the only people who can hire a Rothbardian security force are those who have the money to afford such protection. Since, apparently, only adults can join or employ protection agencies, what happens when some of these parents abuse their children? Who will protect these children from their parents when only the parents have the resources to secure protection? Should the prosecution of child abuse or murder be left to Rothbard's free market? Furthermore, Rothbard's state of nature appears to allow the more wealthy the opportunity to buy more mercenaries or hire more powerful protection agencies. Rothbard's professed concern for human rights seems a bit nearsighted. Clearly, many in a Rothbardian state of nature would suffer from severe disadvantages that would have serious effects upon their rights.

The plausibility of anarchism must be judged in terms of its relevance to the real world. It does little good to fantasize about the possibility of anarchism on an isolated island or in some long lost paradise. Anarchism could undoubtedly work in a utopia where all men had angelic natures or on a small scale in situations where there is no serious or vicious competition for scarce resources, such as a family where mutual love and trust could find voluntary ways to solve problems. But can anarchism work in a world where key resources are scarce and subject to intense and frequently violent competition? Can anarchism succeed in a world where human nature is at best less than benevolent, and at worst, capable of the most dreadful acts of aggression? Can anarchism work in a world where other nations covet greater power and teiritorial expansion and possess the armament to either annihilate their victims or reduce them to total subjugation? The whole point to anarchism is freedom. But it is difficult to be free when one has been conquered by a totalitarian State. It is even more difficult to be free when one is dead!

The anarchistic attack on the State appears more plausible than it really is because it confuses the difference between a necessary evil and a necessary evil. The State is a necessary evil in the same sense as an operation to remove an inflamed appendix. There is nothing especially nice about having one's abdomen opened with a knife. But surgery in such a circumstance is certainly preferable to the alternative. The evil

27

of the surgery is necessary in order to prevent
even greater evils. However, it is possible for
any necessary evil to become a necessary evil. The
surgeon performing the appendectomy may be incom-
petent and may make a serious mistake. Similarly,
given the nature of the men who operate the State,
it is all too easy for the necessary evil of the
State to degenerate into a necessary evil. The
anarchist argument is based on the premise that
the State must always be a necessary evil, that it
is impossible for the State to be anything but an
immoral aggressor against human rights. However,
as dangerous as the institution of the State is,
it will frequently make more sense to gamble with
the State than to face the certain odds of even
greater evils without the State.

THE FOUNDING FATHERS AND THE STATE

The attitude of the American Founding Fathers
toward the State is instructive at this point.
While they were not anarchists, they clearly
recognized the dangers of the State. Even though
they believed government is necessary to control
human passions and selfishness, government itself
can become a menace should it grow too strong.
The proper balance between freedom and order
requires sufficient governmental power to suppress
criminal activity while at the same time insuring
that too much political power is not concentrated
in the hands of a few men. This ideal, Evans
writes,

> has proved, down through the centuries, to be
> quite a task. There is very little diffi-
> culty in establishing either the authoritar-
> ian's contrary ideal of complete (if there-
> fore temporary) freedom. The great problem
> is to set up a system of 'free government,'
> providing both order and freedom.[56]

The political system outlined in the American Constitution gave proper expression to the major
concerns of both freedom and order.

In a word, the model answer to the dilemma of 'free government' is the American Constitution.... It is noteworthy that neither the 'authoritarian' ideas of Hamilton nor the 'libertarian' notions of Jefferson dominated the Constitution. Instead, the great conceptual balance struck by Madison prevailed in that document, and, for a time, in the nation.[57]

The framers of the Constitution had their reasons for wanting to limit the power of government. History had taught them only too clearly about the tendency of the State to become a major instrument in depriving men of liberty. "To expect self-denial from men," John Adams wrote,

> when they have a majority in their favor and consequently power to gratify themselves is to disbelieve all history and universal experience; it is to disbelieve Revelation and the Word of God, which informs us the heart is deceitful in all things and desperately wicked.

Because they believed that human nature could not be trusted, they created a complicated and cumbersome system of government in which various checks and balances serve to make the attainment of absolute power by any one man or group of men extremely difficult. As James Madison observed,

> It may be a reflection on human nature, that such devices [as checks and balances] should be necessary to control the abuses of government. But what is government itself, but the greatest of all reflections on human nature? If men were angels, no government would be necessary. If angels were to govern men, neither external nor internal controls on government would be necessary.[58]

But, of course, men are not angels, and since a government must be established, it must be a government which cannot abuse its authority. In

Madison's words, "You must first enable the government to control the governed; and in next place oblige it to control itself."

One of the more obvious signs of the Framer's belief in a minimal State was the Constitution's clear restriction of the powers of the Federal Government. The Constitution did this, first, by enumerating the only powers actually granted to the central government;[59] secondly, by listing specified prohibitions;[60] and thirdly, by declaring in words too plain to be misunderstood that all powers not expressly delegated to the Federal Government were then reserved to the States and the people. Power must be diffused between both the central and state governments. The Federalist commented on this division between the central and local government:

> In the compound republic of America, the power surrendered by the people is first divided between two distinct governments, and then the portion allotted to each subdivided among distinct and separate departments. Hence, a double security arises to the rights of the people. The different governments will control each other at the same time that each will be controlled by itself.[61]

Frank Meyer expressed a fundamental conviction of contemporary American conservatism when he wrote that the synthesis of freedom and order in the United States Constitution

> was the closest that human beings have come to establishing a policy which gives the possibility of maintaining at one and the same time individual liberty, underlying norms of law, and necessary public order.[62]

Nineteenth century liberals like John Stuart Mill believed government should be limited because men are essentially good. The American Founding Fathers believed that government should be limited because men are essentially evil. Consequently, they developed a political system in which bad men can do the least amount of harm.

THE MINIMAL STATE

Anarchism hardly seems a live option for reasonable people living in the real world. But the falsity of anarchism should not detract from the seriousness of its warnings about the very real dangers of the State. Even if the State must exist, the type of State most compatible with liberty would seem to be a minimal or limited State.

The minimal State to which I refer is <u>not</u> identical to the Night Watchman State of nineteenth century liberalism. The classical liberal State had only three basic functions: (1) the protection of its citizens from the threat of foreign invasion; (2) the protection of the rights of its citizens from violence or fraud or other wrongful interference; (3) the provision of a recognized authority with sufficient force to judge in conflicts between the rights of individuals. The minimal State of which I write has functions that go beyond national defense and the provision of law and order. Since laws must be changed to fit changing conditions, there must be a way in which the rules by which society operates can be changed. There must also be some way of settling disagreements over the meaning of the rules. It is important to notice the additional roles that strong anti-statists like Friedrich Hayek and Milton Friedman are willing to assign to their minimal State. For example, Friedman writes,

A government which maintained law and order, defined property rights, served as a means whereby we could modify property rights and other rules of the economic game, adjudicated disputes about the interpretations of the rules, enforced contracts, promoted competition, provided a monetary framework, engaged in activities to counter technical monopolies and to overcome neighborhood effects widely

31

regarded as sufficiently important to justify government intervention, and which supplemented private charity and the private family in protecting the irresponsible, whether madman or child--such a government would clearly have important functions to perform.[63]

In his latest book, Hayek affirms,

> we find it unquestionable that in an advanced society government ought to use its power of raising funds by taxation to provide a number of services which for various reasons cannot be provided, or cannot be provided adequately, by the market.[64]

Hayek specifically mentions as examples of such legitimate services the counteraction of such neighborhood effects as pollution, the building of roads, the provision of information and standards of measurement, and protection against natural disasters. However, Hayek does note that

> contrary to an assumption often tacitly made, the fact that some services must be financed by compulsory levies by no means implies that such services should also be administered by government. Once the problem of finance is solved, it will often be the more effective method to leave the organization and management of such services to competitive enterprise and rely on appropriate methods of apportioning the funds raised by compulsion among the producers in accordance with some expressed preference of the users.[65]

Amplifications of this outline of the minimal or limited State will recur throughout the rest of this book. My own view approximates the positions of Hayek and Friedman. Since the minimal State they describe serves both the individual and society, their position appears basically compatible with Nisbet's society-affirming State. The minimal State recognizes and respects the fact that its power must not negate the important role that voluntary communities play with regard to the individual.

CHAPTER TWO

JUSTICE

The most effective weapon in the statist's arsenal has been the appeal to social justice. States frequently justify the forcible imposition of new social policy on the ground that it is mandated by the demands of social justice. Especially paradoxical is the picture of totalitarian states proclaiming "social justice" as their most important end at the same time that they pursue a criminal reign of terror against every basic human right.

Robert Nozick, a philosopher at Harvard, is the author of a recent and important book that challenges views of justice that require too great a dependence on the machinery of the State. Statists insist that a minimal State is impotent to deal with most problems of distributive justice. But in Nozick's view, "The minimal state is the most extensive state that can be justified. Any state more extensive violates people's rights."[1] Any attempt to justify a more extensive State in order to attain social justice is unfounded and dangerous. The attainment of justice does not require the existence of a super-state.

Some participants in the debate about justice warn about a clever semantic manuever by the statist that makes his case appear much more plausible than it really is. The cunning strategy attempts to obscure the differences between "justice" and "social justice." It allows the statist to slide conveniently between the positive emotive appeal of the first term and the ambiguous, controversial meaning of the second.

35

Friedrich Hayek doubts seriously if the phrase "social justice" means anything. He believes that

> the near-universal acceptance of a belief does not prove that it is valid or even meaningful any more than the general belief in witches or ghosts proved the validity of these concepts. What we have to deal with in the case of 'social justice' is simply a quasi-religious superstition of the kind which we should respectfully leave in peace so long as it merely makes those happy who hold it, but which we must fight when it becomes the pretext of coercing other men... the prevailing belief in 'social justice' is at present probably the gravest threat to most other values of a free civilization.[2]

The word "justice" has no one single meaning. In a few contexts, it may have no meaning at all.

DIFFERENT SENSES OF "JUSTICE"

Several points made in classical discussions of justice have relevance for the contemporary debate. The ancients believed that justice always involves giving a person his due, that to which he has a right. The reason why a person may be due something varies with the situation. A hypothetical person named Jones would be due something in all of the following cases:

(1) If Jones does better work than any other student in the class, he is due the best grade.
(2) If Jones (presumably, in this case, Ms. Jones) is the prettiest contestant in a beauty contest, she is due first prize.
(3) If Jones is the first to finish a race, he is due the prize.
(4) If Jones is promised something by Smith, Jones is due the fulfillment of the promise.

36

(5) If Jones' property is stolen or damaged by Smith, Jones is due whatever reparation is required to restore what he lost.

The what and why of any person's due cannot be reduced to a single formula of the form, to each according to his _____ . Many attempts have been made to complete this phrase with terms like ability, need and achievement. But each of these criteria would fit some situations and not others. However much the determination of a person's due varies with the situation, it seems clear that "the distinctive feature of justice is that it consists in each person's having that to which he has a right."[3] However complex the total analysis of "justice" may become, any adequate inquiry must retain this ancient insight.

One of the great virtues of Aristotle's discussion of justice was his attempt to distinguish the more important meanings of the word. As Aristotle saw it, a person can be said to be just in two quite different senses.[4] The first of these, universal justice, is coextensive with the whole of righteousness, with the whole of virtue. A person is just in the universal sense if he possesses all the proper virtues, if he is moral, if he keeps the laws, which Aristotle thought should accord with virtuous behavior. A soldier who runs away from the enemy during a battle is unjust in this universal sense. So too is a husband who is unfaithful to his wife or who fails to provide for his family. The just man in Aristotle's universal sense is the one who acts virtuously toward others. The Bible also utilizes this universal sense of justice. It is present in Genesis 6:9 where Noah is described as a just man who is perfect in all his ways. In Ezekiel 18:5, the just man is defined as one who does that which is lawful and right. In fact, the vast majority of biblical allusions to justice appear to be examples of justice in the universal sense.[5] A man is just then in the classical universal sense if he is virtuous and keeps the laws of his country (Aristotle), if he keeps the commandments of God (the Old

37

Testament), if he is kind and charitable, if he
provides for his family, if he helps the poor; in
other words, if he manifests the virtues normally
associated with being a moral or righteous person.
But Aristotle recognized that "justice" may
also be used in the sense of particular justice.
In this particular sense, a man is just if he
treats other people fairly, if he does not grasp
after more than he is due. Aristotle distinguished three kinds of particular justice.
(1) Interpersonal relations involving economic
exchanges raise questions of commercial justice.
For example, a merchant who is honest in his deal-
ings is just in this sense. (2) Instances where
some wrong must be made right under either criminal or civil law are occasions for remedial justice. Cases where an innocent individual is found
guilty or where the punishment for an offense is
too severe or too lenient are instances of injustice in this sense. (3) Finally, questions about
distributive justice arise in situations where
some good or some burden is apportioned among
human beings. Such situations are encountered
frequently, as, for example, when a parent divides
the evening dessert among the members of a large
family or a man divides his estate among his
heirs. As used in contemporary writings, social
justice is that species of distributive justice
concerned with the distribution of burdens and
benefits within society as a whole, a distribution
that is usually controllable by political authorities.

JUSTICE AND EQUALITY

Many people think that justice and equality are
equivalent. Contemporary Liberals view equality
as an unqualified good. Richard Wollheim calls
equality "the fundamental principle of Liberalism."[6] J. Salwyn Schapiro agrees and goes on to
add that "Liberalism has proclaimed the principle
of equality for all human beings everywhere."[7]
This categorical approval of equality was not
nearly so widespread in nineteenth century

liberalism. The French author of Democracy in
America, Alexis de Tocqueville, foresaw the possibility that the ever-widening concern for equality
in America could blur important distinctions in
human talent. He warned of the possibility that a
majority of citizens might achieve economic and
social equality at the cost of conformity in taste
and thought. Such equality would also conflict
with freedom. If the State is to guarantee that
people are equal, it will have to interfere in the
lives of men, often using coercion when they are
unwilling to submit to the State's plan. One of
the basic human liberties, de Tocqueville believed,
was the freedom to be different from other people.
How can this freedom be compatible with a state-
imposed egalitarianism? De Tocqueville also
pointed out one major reason for the popularity of
egalitarian measures. While the value of egalitarian acts always appears rather quickly, it
often takes a great deal of time for the resultant
abuses of freedom to become apparent.

The Liberal's ideological attachment to
equality may account for the infrequency with
which his convictions are supported with arguments. As Nozick observes,

> The legitimacy of altering social institu-
> tions to achieve greater equality of material
> condition is, though often assumed, rarely
> argued for.... It cannot merely be assumed
> that equality must be built into any theory
> of justice. There is a surprising dearth of
> arguments for equality capable of coming to
> grips with the considerations that underlie
> a...nonpatterned conception of justice in
> holdings. (However, there is no lack of
> unsupported statements of a presumption in
> favor of equality.)[8]

As before, the writings of Aristotle are a
good place to begin an exploration of the relationship between justice and equality. For Aristotle, the basic principle of all just actions (in
the particular sense) is summarized in the

statement that equals should be treated equally
and unequals unequally. Injustice always exists
when similar people are treated differently or
when dissimilars are treated alike. Chaim Perelman has referred to Aristotle's formula as the
Formal Principle of Justice.[9] While the Formal
Principle is, many believe, a necessary condition
for any just action, its admirers are quick to
admit the deficiencies of the principle. For one
thing, it is not a sufficient principle of justice. That is, conformity to it will not guarantee justice. For example, a society might decide
to treat all members of a particular class alike,
but badly. Like treatment of likes can be unjust
if the criteria by which people are grouped into
classes are discriminatory and irrelevant to their
claims to justice. The most serious weakness of
the so-called Formal Principle of Justice is the
absence of a criterion to identify which of the
many ways in which people can be compared are
relevant to questions of justice. If one is judg-
ing a beauty contest or assigning grades in a
philosophy class or deciding the winner of an
election, the factors that should count in each
case are both different and fairly obvious. It is
unlikely that a young lady's inability to write a
good philosophy essay will disqualify her from a
beauty contest whereas size 15 feet might. Something else must be added to the Formal Principle
to complete the picture of justice and identify
the relevant respects in which similarities
require similar treatment. Aristotle believed
that human equality and inequality should count
only in instances where the similarity or difference is relevant. While the parentage of a flute-
player is not relevant to the distribution of
flutes, musical ability is. It is not enough to
add up the ways in which human beings are equal or
unequal. One must count only those respects that
are relevant to what is being distributed. Aristotle's discussion suggests that "equality" may be
as slippery a term as "freedom" and "justice."
Aristotle's principle leaves open the possibility
of discriminatory treatment. Similar people in
similar situations should be treated alike. But

the presence of relevant differences also mandates different treatment. Left unstated is a principle to identify which differences should count as grounds for unequal treatment.

In an effort to supplement the Formal Principle, some philosophers have sought a Material Principle of Justice that would supply criteria for justifying dissimilar treatment. A number of these proposed material principles are clearly inadequate. For example, many possible bases of unequal treatment are unacceptable because they are factors for which no one can claim responsibility or credit. This consideration would rule out all attempts to ground a distribution on criteria like sex, race, height, or eye color. Other possible criteria for unequal treatment like wealth, power, and social position should be disqualified because they depend upon earlier distributions which themselves may have been unjust. No theory of distribution can be acceptable which is based upon some feature the possession of which may have resulted from unjust human action. Clearly, a person's sex or race or wealth or power or social position or eye color should not be used as the basis on which he or she receives a larger or smaller share of what is distributed.

The most promising candidates for a material principle of justice are well-known. They include such factors as ability, past achievement, effort, need, merit, and desert. Depending on the context, the application of any of these criteria might be correct. If it is medical care that is being distributed, the health needs of the patient are relevant. If a parent is distributing praise to his children, the deeds or effort of the child are relevant. The distribution of wages is often pertinent to a laborer's work. Great mischief results from the attempt to elevate any one of these principles to the exclusion of the other. Nicholas Rescher observes that all monistic theories recognize but one solitary, homogeneous mode of claim production (be it need, effort, productivity or whatever), to the exclusion of all others. A single, specific ground of claim establishment is canonized as uniquely authoritative, and all the others dismissed. As a result, these canons all suffer the aristocratic fault of hyperexclusiveness.[10]

No single all-embracing material principle of distribution is adequate. Sometimes need is relevant, but not always. Sometimes, but not always, merit should count.

The unsoundness of all attempts to push one exclusive principle invalidates need as the dominant factor affecting dissimilar distributions. Sometimes inequalities based on need are just; but many times they are not. A just distribution of grades for a college course should have nothing to do with whether a student "needs" a particular grade. In this case, the just grade should be assigned on the basis of what the student has earned, not what he needs. The notion of "need" is extremely ambiguous. People "need" things for many different reasons. A student may feel he needs a particular grade in order to qualify for the football team, in order to graduate, in order to continue on the dean's list, so as to qualify for a scholarship, to increase the student's self-esteem. However much sympathy such needs may generate, they should not be relevant in cases like this. If need is to function as one of the several material principles of justice, society must find some way of identifying the essential needs in the given situation. Needs have a way of growing as people become accustomed to former luxuries. A good society will not allow certain fundamental and essential human needs to go unmet while a surplus exists. Whether the efforts of such a society should be described in terms of justice or charity, however, is another matter. Attention, however, should be directed to the unremitting efforts of the statist to expand continually the scope of these "basic needs" so as to justify the

the aggrandizement of statist powers.

The American philosopher, George Mavrodes, notes one important consideration that precludes "any simple passage from justice to equality, or vice versa."

Any policy or pattern of action which we can plausibly defend or recommend on the grounds of equality can also be plausibly attacked and rejected on the grounds of inequality.... if equality is applied to unequals the results are unequal. But human beings and their works are the locus of profound inequalities. Any policy, therefore, which is from one point of view a policy of equal treatment must be from another point of view a sort of unequal treatment. So, if equal opportunities are provided to people with unequal abilities, then the results will predictably be unequal. If, on the other hand, one assigns opportunities in such a way as to generate equal results, then there must be inequalities in the allotment of the opportunities. This sort of factor seems almost painfully evident in the controversies surrounding the recent Bakke case, and the policy of preferential college admissions in general. Each side defends its own preferred policy in terms of equality, and attacks that of its adversary in terms of its inequality.[11]

Mavrodes' remarks suggest the importance of distinguishing between an egalitarianism of results and an egalitarianism of means. To the extent that any State attempts to produce equal results, it will have to treat people differently. But if the egalitarian abandons his quest for equal results and concentrates instead on equal treatment (means), he must then be content with the unequal results that will follow. As Mavrodes observes, "there is not, and cannot be, any public policy which generates equality along all of the important dimensions in which we have an interest."[12]

A position advanced by another American philosopher, William Frankena, is an attempt to resolve the difficulties of attaining equal results. Frankena advocates an egalitarianism that would help people who differ widely in important respects to make the same relative advance to the good life. As he explains, "Matters are to be so disposed ... that everyone has an equal chance of achieving the best life he is capable of."[13] Frankena would have society treat people equally in the sense that it would make the same proportionate contribution to each person's attainment of the best possible life. Frankena's egalitarianism does not attempt to give everyone the same start or even help them reach the same goal. It recognizes the fundamental inequalities among human beings and simply urges that the State help each person make the same relative development.

Most forms of egalitarianism tend to a type of social levelling. Because some people can never be elevated to the level of those with superior intelligence or ability or greater motivation, the concern for equality frequently results in the most gifted being forced to a lower level. Frankena points out how harmful this is to society over the long run. While each person should be given an equal chance to enjoy the best possible life, it is sometimes necessary to give extra attention to the especially gifted. Since the gifted are often people who lead society, aiding them helps all within society. At the very least, society should place no obstacles in the path of the more gifted. In a free society where people are not restrained from helping themselves, the gifted will naturally be better achievers. Those who argue that it is unjust for society to do anything extra for gifted individuals who are able to achieve a better life, until all have been brought up to their highest level, ignore the role that the gifted can play in raising the level of the rest of society. Frankena also criticizes attempts to understand equality in an exclusively materialistic sense. He believes society should be more concerned with promoting a level of quality of life.

Frankena's egalitarianism is certainly more sensible and more responsible than that of many contemporaries. But it is doubtful that even his severely restricted interpretation of equality will withstand careful scrutiny. Frankena realizes the absurdity of attempts to give everyone an equal start and the immorality of efforts to guarantee an equal finish. But is even his more restricted goal of aiding everyone to make equal progress really possible? How can any State ever know if all the members of a society are making equal progress? In order for the State to make the same proportionate contribution to each individual's relative advance to the good life, the State would require more knowledge than any State could possibly or rightfully obtain. Frankena's model would also require a massive amount of statist intervention into the everyday affairs of the society. The State would require precise information about where each person starts genetically, environmentally, intellectually, financially, and how each is progressing toward his or her goals. Some people grow by choice and effort. Others stagnate. Some will get worse no matter what the State does for them. In fact, considerable evidence exists that as some classes become dependent on State support, they experience a weakening of motivation. How can the State help everyone make a proportional advance when some care nothing about improvement? If Frankena has been misunderstood and he only intends to recommend that the State make provision for minimal standards of education, of life and of security, his proposals would appear consistent with the minimal State.

What is the sum of all this? The equating of justice and equality presumed by several contempoary ideologies is unjustified. Sometimes equal treatment is just, often it is not. The two concepts are not equivalent. Frequently, justice will require that people be treated differently. Many egalitarian programs are either totally

45

impractical and/or dangerous as they justify
greater expansions of statist power.

PATTERN VS. PROCESS THEORIES OF JUSTICE

One of the more important advances in understanding the concept of justice has been Robert
Nozick's suggestion that a distinction be drawn
between End-Result and Historical theories of justice. End-Result theories are forward-looking in
the sense "that the justice of a distribution is
determined by how things are distributed (who has
what) as judged by some structural principle(s) of
just distribution."[14] Historical approaches to
justice look backwards. They "hold that past circumstances or actions of people can create differential entitlements or differential deserts to
things."[15] For Nozick who advocates the Historical approach, justice does not depend on some
social arrangement having consequences of a certain kind. Justice is tied rather to past and
present considerations.

Nozick focuses his attention on one major
representative of the End-Result and the Historical approaches to justice. He notes that many
End-Result theories attempt to locate justice in
some pattern of distribution.

Proponents of patterned principles of distributive justice focus upon criteria for
determining who is to receive holdings; they
consider the reasons for which someone should
have something, and also the total picture of
holdings. Whether or not it is better to
give than to receive, proponents of patterned
principles ignore giving altogether. In con-
sidering the distribution of goods, income,
and so forth, their theories are theories of
recipient justice; they completely ignore any
right a person might have to give something
to someone.... Patterned principles of distributive justice necessitate redistributive
activities. The likelihood is small that any

46

actual freely-arrived-at set of holdings fits a given pattern; and the likelihood is nil that it will continue to fit the pattern as people exchange and give.[16]

According to this view, if a particular distribution matches a pre-conceived pattern (and there are several possible patterns that might be adopted), then it is just. It makes no difference who the recipients are; nor does it matter if that which they receive is due them. All that counts is that the actual distribution fit the pattern. For example, egalitarians approach questions of justice with the assumption that a just distribution will tend toward a pattern of equality. When a political Liberal talks about distributive justice on a societal level, he usually has three things in mind. First, he believes his society's present distribution is unjust because it fails to measure up to his pre-conceived pattern of how goods and burdens ought to be distributed. Secondly, he believes the present spread must be altered to match better his criterion. And finally, the required redistribution cannot be voluntary. Because the more privileged members of society will not willingly part with their greater share, the Liberal wants the State to be authorized to take by force whatever the central authority believes necessary to meet the requirements of "justice." That this appropriation is normally effected through taxation does not, of course, alter the fact that it is an act of force.

Nozick's own proposal, a type of Historical approach to justice, is called The Entitlement Theory of Justice. Nozick believes that pattern theories ignore ethically relevant factors in the past history of how people came to their present holdings, factors that are pertinent to what each person is due. Nozick urges that little attention be paid to the final pattern of distribution. What marks the holdings of people as just or unjust is not who holds what, but how each person acquired his holdings through a process of original acquisition and transfer. If a person is entitled to

47

his holdings because its original acquisition was just and because the subsequent transfers that led to his holding were just, then he and others like him are entitled to their holdings and the distribution is just regardless of its pattern. Nozick distinguishes between a person's being entitled to a holding and deserving that holding. A person might have inherited money which he did not deserve. But his lack of desert does not weaken the fact that he is entitled to his wealth.

Two of Nozick's criticisms of pattern theories of justice will be noted. First, such attempts rest upon a misleading analogy. Distributive justice is a meaningful concept in many commonly encountered situations. Several examples were mentioned earlier: the decision confronting a parent about to divide the evening dessert within a family where the members differ considerably in size, age, needs, and hunger; a testator preparing his will; a university administrator who has x number of dollars to divide among a group of faculty as their raises for the next year.

Such paradigm cases have certain features in common. They are controlled situations in the sense that they are fairly limited in size and scope. The distributors have some legitimate claim to that which they are distributing and can usually, at least in principle, obtain the relevant information needed to come to a decision. For example, the parent about to divide the pie can ask how hungry everyone is. In such controlled everyday situations, the concept of distributive justice makes perfectly good sense.

However, a massive leap is required to get from the limited and controlled situations where considerations of distributive justice are obviously relevant to the unlimited and spontaneous situations found in society as a whole. In limited situations, justice is possible because the distributor usually has access to the information he needs to make his decisions. But when the context becomes as broad as an entire society, no one person or central authority can ever attain sufficient knowledge about the millions of individuals and the incalculable number of decisions, actions, and exchanges that have brought them to their present holdings. The more complex a society, the less likely it is that any one person or central agency can possess all the essential information. When the whole of society is in view, Nozick contends,

> we are not in the position of children who have been given portions of pie by someone who now makes last minute adjustment to rectify careless cutting. There is no central distribution, no person or group entitled to control all the resources, jointly deciding how they are to be doled out. What each person gets, he gets from others who give to him in exchange for something, or as a gift. In a free society, diverse persons control different resources, and new holdings arise out of the voluntary exchanges and actions of persons.... The total result is the product of many individual decisions which the different individuals involved are entitled to make.[17]

The analogy between the limited situations in which distributive justice makes sense and the unlimited spontaneous situation that characterizes society as a whole is misleading for two reasons: first, because sufficient information in the case of a whole society is unattainable; and secondly, because no central authority really has a right to the things it usually distributes. As one of Nozick's commentators explains,

> Resources, Nozick insists, are not manna from heaven, requiring to be distributed by some person or group entitled to control the distribution; they are already distributed as a result of many individual transactions in the past, just or unjust. The assumption that there is a problem of distribution is the

fundamental mistake of all theories of justice whose basic concern is to determine 'who ends up with what.'18

Nozick's first objection to pattern theories of justice, then, is the claim that their appeal to social justice is based upon a false analogy between a just distribution in a limited controlled situation and a just distribution in an unlimited spontaneous situation.

Nozick's second objection is that pattern theories are incompatible with freedom. This can easily be seen by imagining a society marked by four conditions: (1) assume that any one of the several popular patterns of distributive justice has been successfully imposed on an entire society. For our purposes, it does not matter which particular pattern it is. It might be a pattern of equal distribution (whatever that should turn out to mean) or distribution according to need; or any other theory. (2) Suppose that the citizens are free to exchange or transfer their holdings in any way they choose. (3) Assume that any appropriation of another person's holdings by theft, force, fraud or other criminal activity will be recognized as unjust and forbidden by law. (4) Finally, in order to eliminate an essentially irrelevant objection, assume that this society contains no persons who are unable to produce or exchange. Therefore, in any society where our conditions are met, any non-criminal voluntary transfer or exchange of holdings like property or money will be a just transfer. That is, if we assume that the original holdings of everyone in the initial situation (the situation obtaining immediately after the patterned distribution) are just because they match the preconceived pattern of distributive justice, and if all subsequent transfers are just, then any deviation from the original pattern of holdings will be just, no matter how much it departs from the original pattern.19 In any free society, it would not take long for new holdings to vary greatly from the original pattern of distribution. This situation would confront the

50

defenders of that original pattern with three options. (1) They might be sensible and realize that even though great discrepancies in holdings now exist, the disparity resulted from voluntary, legal, and just exchanges. And so even though the later situation no longer resembles the preferred pattern of distribution, the situation must be judged just and no further meddling with the new distribution is justified.

(2) What is more likely, given the mind-set of the ideologues, is that after a certain period of time, they would announce that the distribution is once again unacceptable, which fact would require the State to step in to rectify the situation. The use of words like "rectify" or "make right" in this context are certainly odd since nothing immoral, criminal or unjust occurred. How can there be anything to rectify? The example makes it clear that appeals to rectification in such cases have little to do with justice or morality. The term simply provides another excuse for statist redistribution. But suppose, following the second establishment of the preferred pattern, the people are once again left free to do what they wish with their possessions. Similar deviations from the preferred pattern would soon reappear. And so the State would have to intervene again and again. Note that at the time of each redistribution, people who had acquired holdings honestly and fairly would be deprived of them without recourse; and this would be done in the name of justice.

(3) Should the State eventually tire of constantly forcing periodic redistributions, it could pursue the third possible course of action. It could simply deprive the citizens of the freedom to transfer and exchange their holdings at will. That is, the State could intrude into the everyday affairs of each citizen and control each and every action. As Nozick warns,

no end-state principle of justice can be continously realized without continuous inter-

51

ference with people's lives. Any favored pattern would be transformed into one unfavored by the principle, by people choosing to act in various ways; for example, by people exchanging goods and services with other people, or giving things to other people, things the transferrers are entitled to under the favored distributional pattern. To maintain a pattern one must either continually interfere to stop people from transferring resources as they wish to, or continually (or periodically) interfere to take from some persons resources that others for some reason chose to transfer to them.[20]

Social justice, as viewed by statist proponents of pattern approaches, is possible only in a society that is controlled from the top down. There must be a central agency with the power to force people to accept the preferred pattern of distribution. And because people's normal desires will lead them to exchanges that will upset the original pattern, the pattern can only be preserved by continuous interference with the lives of its citizens. If social justice is to have any meaning, any factors that might contribute to spontaneous deviations from the desired pattern must be eliminated. It is understandable how Friedrich Hayek could speak of social justice as "the Trojan Horse through which totalitarianism has entered many societies in the world."[21]

The statist assumes that his promotion of social justice simply means the addition of a new moral value to those known in the past. He believes this new moral value "can be fitted within the existing framework of moral rules. What is not sufficiently recognized is that in order to give [social justice] meaning a complete change of the whole character of the social order will have to be effected, and that some of the values which used to govern it will have to be sacrificed." Hayek fears that "like most attempts to pursue an unattainable goal, the striving for [social justice] will also produce highly undesirable consequences, and in particular lead to the destruction of the indispensable environment in which the traditional moral values alone can flourish, namely personal freedom."[22]

JUST RESULTS OR JUST PROCEDURES

As already noted, attempts to view justice as a property of the end-result of social interaction face serious problems. Several contemporary thinkers have proposed instead that justice be seen as a property of procedures. Three distinctions made in John Rawls' book, A Theory of Justice,[23] provide a helpful introduction to the contrast between just results and just procedures. Rawls differentiates between: (1) perfect procedural justice; (2) imperfect procedural justice; and (3) pure procedural justice. The first two types of procedural justice hold in common the belief that it is possible to identify the justice or injustice of the result of a distribution independently of the procedure that was followed. In the last case, pure procedural justice, it is impossible to know which particular results will be just; it is only possible to know what would constitute a just procedure to follow. The difference between (1) and (2) turns, once the "just" result is determined, on whether or not some procedure is available that will guarantee the desired result.

(1) Perfect procedural justice is possible only in situations where the specific end-result is identified as just and where some procedure is available that will guarantee precisely that pattern. The example Rawls cites is that of cutting a cake. If it is assumed that the most just result will be a division of the cake into equal pieces, it is relatively easy to prescribe a procedure that will produce equal pieces, namely, require that the last piece on the plate goes to the person cutting the cake. If the cake-cutter wishes the largest possible piece for himself, he will have to cut the cake into equal pieces.

53

(2) Rawls' example of imperfect procedural justice is a criminal trial. Its goal is to convict the guilty and to set the innocent free. What will constitute a just result in this instance, then, is known. Unfortunately, no trial procedure is known that will always produce the just verdict. Innocent people are found guilty and the guilty are set free with embarrasing frequency. Even though a correct verdict may result most of the time, the potential for error is always present. Even at their best, criminal trials are examples of imperfect procedural justice.

(3) Pure procedural justice differs from (1) and (2) in that there is no separate criterion for a just result. Instead, Rawls points out, "there is a correct or fair procedure such that the outcome is likewise correct or fair, whatever it is, provided that the procedure has been properly followed."[24] In other words, pure procedural justice applies in cases where there is no way of specifying or knowing in advance what a just result would be. All one can do is try and make the procedures as just as possible. Then, whatever results from those just procedures must be recognized as just. Rawls' example is gambling. If the gamblers keep the rules, if there is no cheating, then the result, whatever it turns out to be, is just. Obviously, a gambler victimized by loaded dice or a doped race horse or a bribed umpire can plead the injustice of the outcome. But if the procedures agreed to in advance are followed fairly, any loser's complaint about the injustice of his loss is empty rhetoric.

Rawls' three types of procedural justice serve as models of three approaches to distributive justice. The position of a few fanatical ideologues appears to follow the model of perfect procedural justice. Some militant Marxists, for example, give the impression that they not only know what would constitute a just society (just results) but that they also know precisely what measures (procedures) will guarantee those results.

According to Rawls, utilitarianism as a
social theory approaches justice from the perspective of imperfect procedural justice. The utilitarian has his independent criterion of a just
result, viz., the greatest balance of happiness.
In utilitarian theory, "institutions are more or
less imperfect arrangements for bringing about
this end."[25] As Joel Feinberg explains,

> When we choose from the point of view of
> fairness among various capitalist, socialist,
> and mixed schemes for organizing an economy,
> we cannot hope to find a system that is cer-
> tain to generate a just outcome in every
> instance, giving every citizen exactly his
> due as determined by an independent material
> criterion of distributive justice. Even
> assuming agreement on the criterion of a just
> distributive outcome, our choice is more like
> that between rival procedures for conducting
> a criminal trial.... Similarly, in the choice
> among economic systems on the assumption of
> independent standards for just outcomes, we
> must decide which of the alternative systems
> of procedures will come closest to satisfying
> those standards, subject to the restrictions
> of such other values as efficiency and lib-
> erty.[26]

Anti-statists believe the model of justice
most appropriate to a free economy is pure procedural justice. Even Rawls has kind things to say
about it.

> Now the great practical advantage of pure
> procedural justice is that it is no longer
> necessary in meeting the demands of justice
> to keep track of the endless variety of cir-
> cumstances and the changing relative posi-
> tions of particular persons. One avoids the
> problem of defining principles to cope with
> the enormous complexities which would arise
> if such details were relevant. It is a mis-
> take to focus attention on the varying rela-
> tive positions of individuals and to require

that every change, considered as a single
transaction viewed in isolation, be in itself
just.... A distribution cannot be judged in
isolation from the system of which it is the
outcome or from what individuals have done in
good faith in the light of established expec-
tations. If it is asked in the abstract
whether one distribution of a given stock of
things to definite individuals with known
desires and preferences is better than
another, then there is simply no answer to
this question.27

The system of economic exchanges found in the
free market is analogous to a kind of game. During the course of the game, much can be done to
insure that the conduct of the players will be
fair or just. The rules can be announced and
enforced by impartial officials. But beyond see-
ing that the game is played fairly, nothing in
the nature of justice permits any tinkering with
the final score; nothing can or should be done to
guarantee a "just" result, that is, a score that
is morally satisfying to the spectator. One might
feel that because one of the teams has lost fifty
straight times that it "deserves" to win. But any
cheating on the part of the players or favoritism
on the part of the umpires that would help realize
the "morally preferable" outcome would be unjust.
Once the rules have been agreed upon in advance of
play, any violation of those rules is an injustice. And if the game is played according to the
rules, no one can complain that the final score
was unjust. The Liberal's confusion of economic
and moral merit leads him to want to "fix" the
final score.

While the analogy of the market to a game
serves a useful purpose, it should not be pushed
too far. In the case of games, today's score seldom affects tomorrow's play. If the Cincinnati
Reds beat the Dodgers 21-0 today, they both begin
tomorrow's play dead even. Regrettably, the economic game does not work that way. The economic
game, in a sense, seldom ends and there are many

times when those who have lost remain losers indefinitely; and their losses may affect the ability of their offspring to play the game in the future. To be sure, proponents of the welfare state overstate this problem and ignore the countless thousands who have used the freedom and opportunity of the market to succeed in spite of great handicaps. But what if the market, in spite of the advantages it has brought to the poor of past generations, is incapable of relieving all poverty and need? Should those unable to help themselves be allowed to suffer? Or course not. Friedrich Hayek is quite clear about this:

> There is no reason why in a free society government should not assure to all protection against severe deprivation in the form of an assured minimum income, or a floor below which nobody need to descend. To enter into such an insurance against extreme misfortune may well be in the interest of all; or it may be felt to be a clear moral duty of all to assist, within the organized community, those who cannot help themselves. So long as such a uniform minimum income is provided outside the market to all those who, for any reason, are unable to earn in the market an adequate maintenance, this need not lead to a restriction of freedom, or conflict with the Rule of Law. The problems with which we are here concerned arise only when the remuneration for services rendered is determined by authority, and the impersonal mechanism of the market which guides the direction of individual efforts is thus suspended.[28]

The alleviation of suffering in an affluent society can occur through extra-market means that fall far short of granting the State the added powers statists believe it must have. The details of the ways this might be done can be derived from such works as Hayek's The Constitution of Liberty and Milton Friedman's Capitalism and Freedom.

ECONOMIC MERIT AND MORAL MERIT

Questions of distributive justice could never arise apart from some economic system within which scarce goods can be acquired and exchanged. The economic system produces the pie; it is quite another thing to provide criteria to determine the most just way to cut the pie. Economics itself does not provide the criteria of a just distribution. Economics qua economics deals with the means by which certain ends can be realized; it does not pass judgment on the morality of those ends. Obviously, individual economists make moral judgments all the time. But the market itself does not presume to place any value on human choices. That is the task of moral philosophy and theology which serve as indispensable helpmates for economics. The market provides incentives for people to produce and makes it possible for them to transfer and exchange their holdings. What transpires in the market will be as moral or immoral as the human beings active in the market. The moral criteria that judge those actions and their consequences must come from some discipline other than economics. Because the market itself is amoral and does not supply the moral standards to evaluate what transpires within the system, it is a mistake to confuse economic merit (the value something has in the market) with moral merit. Just because a well-known athlete commands a yearly salary of $500,000, it does not follow that he possesses more moral merit than a poorly paid minister or nurse. What people deserve economically and morally are not the same. There may be good economic reasons for paying a skilled baseball player twenty or thirty times as much as a skilled philosophy teacher, even though the philosopher may be more deserving in a moral sense. The widespread tendency to connect moral and economic merit is to be avoided. Because many people are offended by the fact that someone who is less deserving in a moral sense is worth more economically, they believe steps should be taken to alter the situation through statist action. It is worth noting that there never seem to be enough people

58

willing to alter the situation economically, for example, by paying more to hear the philosopher lecture than to watch the athlete perform.

The socialist attempt to apply moral principles to economic activities leads to a confusion of moral and economic desert. The socialist wishes to replace the market where value depends upon supply and demand with a socio-economic value which rewards moral merit. It is not difficult to organize dissatisfaction with the actual distribution of the market. It is natural to feel moral outrage at the prosperity of the wicked; it is easy to feel envy at the prosperity of the righteous. As long as some have more than others, it is natural for discontent to arise among those with less. But those who believe that statist interference with the market will guarantee the primacy of moral merit are mistaken. Once the distribution is placed in the hands of the State, it is highly likely that moral merit will once again be reduced to second place while the major shares go to reward political merit, as in Marxist countries. The attempt to alleviate the disparities resulting from the market's reward of economic merit could lead to a highly discriminatory and politically biased distribution that is just as much in conflict with a moral perspective. Instead of being rewarded for economic contributions or for moral merit, a person will be rewarded for service to the State.

JUSTICE AND THE WELFARE STATE

No adequate justification for the welfare state has yet been given. This fact is openly acknowledged by the authors of a recent book defending the welfare state. They admit that "The social philosophy behind the welfare state is vague and inchoate."[29] The highly regarded American philosopher, Sidney Hook, concedes that "the absence of a dominant theorist or of a single commanding system of thought endorsing the welfare state has been documented again and again."[30]

59

Even though a plausible case for the welfare state has yet to be made, its supporters contend that the welfare state must be continued because it, more than any rival view of government, "conforms to the elemental standards of justice and decency."[31] This justification does not exactly constitute indisputable evidence.

Several considerations weigh heavily against the welfare state. Attention has already been drawn to such matters as the welfare state's threat to personal liberty. Donald J. Devine notes some of these problems:

> Beyond the problem of whether real welfare is provided and whether this reaches those who deserve it, is the fundamental problem that coercion, including government coercion, can cause injury which is typically feared as the worst injustice which can be inflicted upon a society. Government injury may be done to those who are forced to contribute so that others may have more goods or services, or to those who are forced to behave in a certain manner so that others may have a congenial environment and social companionship.[32]

Devine goes on to note that "not only may those perceived to be giving be harmed but those perceived to be receiving also may be aggrieved-- either because by stating that the problem has been solved by government, alternative assistance is not given; or as a result of an injury from an intended or, more often, an unintended consequence of this or another government policy."[33] In other words, evidence exists that welfare state policies do more than injure those from whom something is taken; they also injure those to whom something is given. Liberal housing programs did not make more low-cost housing available for the poor; the result has been much less available housing, at a cost of billions of dollars. Minimum wage legislation does not really help people at the bottom of the economic ladder; it ends up

harming them by making them less employable, thus
increasing unemployment among the very people the
legislation is supposed to help.   The short-
sighted and politically expedient policy of paying
for social welfare through deficit spending has
flooded the economy with billions of dollars of
increasingly worthless money and ravaged the poor
by subjecting them (and everyone else) to an
inflation that continues to raise the prices of
basic necessities beyond their reach. Regardless
of where one looks, welfare state programs have
failed.

After four decades of experience, then,
the promises of the welfare state have not
been realized and, indeed, its costs have
been immense. Not only have hundreds of billions of dollars in national wealth been
squandered which could have been used for
constructive social purposes but there have
been staggering social costs as well. Hundreds of thousands of youth, and especially
minority youth, have been made unemployed or
underemployed through minimum wage and related employment laws; millions of children are
taught values their parents object to and
thousands of children are transported out of
their neighborhoods while the poorer support
the better-off to obtain more income and
higher education. At the same time, almost
everyone is forced to pay more dearly for
medical and hospital care in the name of medical care for all while, at the cost of tens
of billions of dollars, housing programs have
resulted in less and more costly housing for
the poor. In addition, even food and clothing essentials have been made more difficult
to obtain for those most in need as a direct
and indirect result of government regulation
while everyone's savings have been ravaged by
inflation.[34]

Liberal social policies have done the most
harm in basic areas like food and clothing. The
people who have been hurt the most have been those

61

least able to afford it, the very people, the Liberal assures us, whom he is trying to help. Clear and Present Dangers, a recent book by M. Stanton Evans, is a powerful, documented indictment of the counter-productiveness of Liberal social action.[35]

Of course, claims like these run contrary to the tide of contemporary political "wisdom." Advocates of the welfare state argue that if their efforts have fallen short of their humanitarian goals, it is because obstinate apologists for the status quo kept the Liberal State from attaining all of the powers it needed. In spite of all the power concentrated in the State and in spite of all the Liberal failures, these miscarriages are offered as reasons for giving the State even greater influence, rather than as evidence for calling the Liberal view into question.

It is inconceivable to many Liberals that any social problem might not have an answer, or that some answers might lie in the private sector. It is unthinkable that human reason could fail to discover some plan that would make things better. If a social problem exists, something--anything-- must be done. Liberals love to present themselves as the great advocates of progress. For them, nothing is worse than standing still or doing nothing. Change, any change, is better than nothing. The Liberal mania for change has reminded some of a caged hamster madly turning the wheel in its cage faster and faster. In neither case, that of the hamster or the Liberal, does the abundance of motion produce any progress. Many Liberals are also persuaded that they are morally superior to their opponents. After all, they want society to be better. Those who oppose their sincere efforts to improve society by statist measures must therefore lack their high ideals. Regrettably, what usually passes for virtuous social action in Liberal theory is little more than bad economics. Any economics whose recommended means to a particular goal result in the realization of a contrary goal is bad economics. Economic policies that end up injuring the very people they are supposed to

62

help are bad policies. A perverse and misguided utopianism has pervaded entirely too much social and political thought in recent decades. Many statists seem always to be chasing rainbows and insisting that all of society be mobilized to help realize their dreams. Unfortunately, time and money spent pursuing unattainable goals divert resources that might have accomplished more had they been used in other ways. Grandiose promises that could never be kept foster disillusionment, despair, and resentment.

Consider how the Liberal's obsession with the proper distribution of society's goods blinds him to a crucial truth: that before society can have enough to distribute among the needy, a sufficient quantity of goods must be produced. By focusing all their attention on who gets what, defenders of the welfare state promote policies that severely restrict production. Advocates of the welfare state paint a picture of an unending flow of cash from the producers in society to the non-producers. But as the sphere of benefits for the non-productive segment of society continues to increase, the mass of marginal producers realizes that the gap between them and welfare recipients is shrinking. Inevitably, they begin to lose their incentive to continue as producers--and as taxpayers. So they give up and join the ever-growing army drawing welfare benefits paid for by the ever-diminishing group of producers. Liberal social policies that continue to drain a society's productive capacities hold ominous implications for the welfare of future generations. This is already apparent in the case of the social security system. A genuine concern for the welfare of future generations should result in economic policies that will encourage a thriving productive base that will allow future generations to meet their own needs and permit them the luxury of supporting their contemporaries who may suffer from deprivation.

One proponent of the welfare state has fairly and accurately articulated a separate concern of many who oppose the system.

> Many people believe that nearly all wel-
> fare programs...reward the irresponsible and
> self-indulgent and penalize the frugal and
> self-sufficient. For example, it is argued
> that self-sufficient middle-class people tend
> to postpone gratification and hence sacrifice
> today for greater benefits tomorrow. Middle-
> class children defer immediate income from
> jobs to attend college. They also defer mar-
> riage and the starting of a family until
> after college. It is further widely believed
> that middle-class families limit the number
> of children they have while lower-class poor
> families do not.... These middle-class tax-
> payers who pay the welfare bills then feel
> aggrieved because they believe they are being
> penalized for limiting the number of children
> they have. They are responsible enough to
> limit the number of their children to those
> they can support, and yet they are also being
> taxed to pay for children on welfare.[36]

It does seem to require a strong dose of ideology
to call such discrimination just. The Equal Education Opportunity Act is a perfect illustration
of such discrimination. Consider two families
with identical incomes for several years. Suppose
one family made numerous sacrifices in order to
acquire savings and a financial security that
would enable it to give its children a college
education. Assume that the other family, with the
same income, failed to practice the conservative
measures of the first family. While it could have
saved as much as the first, it spent its excess
money on expensive vacations and fancy cars. How
does the welfare state reward the sacrifices of
the first family and the extravagances of the
second? It does so by awarding the children of
the second family scholarships it denies to the
first. Is this Liberal justice in action?

Norman Bowie continues:

A second cause of resentment is captured
by the notion of the culture of poverty. It
is argued that once a person is on welfare,
he or she seems content to stay there.
Indeed, the children of persons on welfare
seem to end up on welfare too.... Welfare
payments on families, it is argued, are simply a waste. Give them money and it goes for
booze. Give them a decent home and it will
soon be a wreck. Welfare recipients have
neither the intellectual ability nor the
moral character to use income, food stamps,
or low-income housing as opportunities to get
their feet on the ground and out of poverty.
As a result, welfare recipients are not entitled to a minimum standard of living and
society has no obligation to provide it;
indeed, most of the tax money used for welfare is simply wasted.[37]

Bowie, it must be remembered, supports the welfare
state and is summarizing what he takes to be the
basis for resentment against the system. He does
a good job. Nor can he deny some truth in these
allegations. Bowie counters by arguing that the
last objection ignores important distinctions
within the class of poor people. Some people are
poor for reasons beyond their control or responsibility. They may have been victimized by illness
or some handicap; they may have been orphaned or
widowed; their parents may have failed them; they
may have become unemployed through no fault of
their own. The point is, some poor people do have
hopes and ambition and lack only some assistance
in order to move beyond poverty. Bowie is right;
many of the poor can be helped.

Bowie notes a second class of the poor that
presents more difficulties. This is the group of
poorly motivated poor. In spite of this group's
bad attitudes and the fact that they appear not to
care, the availability of new opportunities might
produce a change of attitudes in some of them.
Thus, while all the members of the first class of
poor people might respond favorably to welfare,

65

only a percentage of the second group will ever be truly helped.

The third and final class of the poor is that group which, Bowie acknowledges, is hopeless. Regardless of what the State does for them, they will never improve. Bowie admits that middle-class resentment appears justified in the case of this third group. But, he argues, there is no way of knowing for sure what percentage of the poor belongs to the irredeemably poor. Nor is there agreement on the justifiable extent to which the middle-class taxpayer should be forced to sacrifice to reach the uncertain percentage in class two that can be helped.

Milton Friedman's welfare proposals retained an important place for incentives. The individual on welfare would be encouraged, and not discouraged, to find employment and move off the welfare rolls. Anti-statist measures would restrict drastically the size of the bureaucracy required to dispense the welfare and reduce the amount of statist intervention into the everyday lives of every citizen, taxpayer and welfare recipient. Repeated Liberal rejections of such measures coupled with the repeated failures of their own programs suggest that the Liberal's real concerns lie in directions other than the provision of help for the needy.

Suppose a member of Congress were to propose a new way of financing America's domestic programs. Imagine proposed legislation that would require each American to pay the same total tax bill that he owes under the present tax structure, the difference being that Washington would keep and disburse only that percentage of the tax-payer's bill that corresponds to the percentage of the federal budget presently allocated to foreign policy and national defense. Suppose the remaining 50-60% of the citizen's tax obligation would still have to be paid, but the taxpayer would be given the freedom to distribute those funds to any domestic programs he chose.[38] The citizen might choose to give a great deal of his domestic tax obligation to organizations devoted to helping the poor or to saving the snail darter. He could support education or any of thousands of programs. It takes little imagination to anticipate Liberal objections to such legislation. Millions of dollars would be wasted on totally worthless projects, the Liberal would no doubt argue. The appearance of a sudden resentment of support for worthless projects on the part of Liberals would be something new for Washington. One would have to be careful of giving examples of such worthless projects since the odds are very high that such a project is already the recipient of federal aid. Another objection would point to the dangers of abuse, to the very real possibilities that people would find ways of cheating the good intentions of the system. This is another curious argument coming from a group singularly unconcerned about the massive abuses of the present system. But the major Liberal opposition to our hypothetical legislation would insist that many worthy projects might go unfunded unless the omni-benevolent and all-knowing State made the decisions. But if the programs were really worthy, it is likely that conscientious citizens could be found to support them. Perhaps if the federal bureaucracy's past record of spending were more responsible, the claim to its moral superiority in the distribution process might be more plausible.

I suspect the real reasons why legislation like this would fail have nothing to do with the greater efficiency of the central planning agency. I believe the proposal would fail, not because it would threaten any deserving program, but because it would deprive the bureaucrats of power. The programs are necessary to the statist, not as a means of aiding the poor, but as a means to his possession of power; and that is what the Liberal State is all about.

The principle beneficiaries of the money absorbed and dispensed by government are not poor blacks in ghettos or Appalachian whites or elderly pensioners receiving Social Security checks--the usual figures conjured up when social welfare is discussed. The major beneficiaries, instead, are the employees of government itself--people engaged in administering some real or imagined service to the underprivileged or, as the case may be, the overprivileged.... The gross effect of increased government spending is to transfer money away from relatively low income people --average taxpayers who must pay the bills-- to relatively high income people--Federal functionaries who are being paid out of the taxpayer's pocket.[39]

As Evans notes further, "the two richest counties in the United States are...Montgomery County, Maryland, and Fairfax County, Virginia--principle bedroom counties for Federal workers in Washington, D.C."[40] It pays to serve the poor under the aegis of the Liberal welfare state.

JOHN RAWLS' THEORY OF JUSTICE

A Theory of Justice by John Rawls has received so much attention since its publication that some evaluation must be included here. Because of its length (607 pages) and complexity, only the quickest summary is possible. It is somewhat ironic that a work acclaimed by many as a modern philosophic classic should nonetheless lead its readers to extremely diverse interpretations. Daniel Bell praised the book as "the most comprehensive effort in modern philosophy to justify a socialistic ethic."[41] The anti-socialist, Friedrich Hayek, believed Rawls to be a supporter of his own type of individualism.[42] The Libertarian philosopher, John Hospers, is convinced that "Rawls' just society turns out to conform to the ideals of a moderately left-leaning member of the Democratic Party."[43] Robert Nozick's Anarchy, State and Utopia criticizes Rawls for holding an end-result theory of justice. And yet Rawls' comments about pure procedural justice, already noted, entail conclusions very compatible with Nozick's view. Rawls regarded his book as a rejection of utilitarian views of justice; yet his own theory of justice appears to be a forward-looking theory that ties justice to the consequences of certain actions. There is deserved punch in the observation of the British philosopher, R. M. Hare, that Rawls' book makes one feel as though his ideas, like sand along the seashore, keep slipping through one's fingers. Drawing attention to the book's many repetitions, Hare notes it is "seldom clear whether the repetitions really are repetitions, or modifications of previously expressed views."44 It is likely that selected passages from Rawls' book could be used in defense of any of the major theories of justice discussed in this chapter. While Rawls' himself is a Liberal with definite statist leanings, his book can be read as supportive of several different theories of justice.

One of the original features of Rawls' book is a device he introduces to support two principles of justice he advocates. The device, similar to the state of nature theory found in the writings of Hobbes, Locke, and Rousseau, requires that anyone desiring to discover the principles needed to make a society just, should imagine himself in an original situation where no State exists. If a group of people, living without a State, had the power to plan for the organization of a State, Rawls thinks it is instructive to note precisely what principles of justice they would select. In order to make the choices of the people in this Rawlsian state of nature more significant, Rawls insists that their knowledge must be limited in a number of important respects. If the people knew what situations they would occupy once the State was organized, it is likely they would vote for principles of justice that would benefit themselves. That is, if they were men, they might vote for principles that would discriminate in favor of men. If they were in line for a large inheritance, their principles of justice might rule out or minimize inheritance taxes. If they

knew they were going to be poor or handicapped,
they might favor principles of justice that would
work to the advantage of people in these classes.
Therefore, Rawls draws down what he calls "the
veil of ignorance." We must assume, he says,
that the people in the state of nature know nothing about their wealth, talents, occupations,
race, sex, or anything else that might prejudice
their selection of the principles of justice.
Once the slate is wiped clean, once people in
theory know absolutely nothing about their personal destiny in the new society, the principles
of justice are exactly the principles any rational
people would select, if they were indeed behind a
veil of ignorance. From his original situation,
Rawls adopts two principles of justice.

> First: each person is to have an equal
> right to the most extensive basic liberty
> compatible with a similar liberty for others.
> Second: social and economic inequalities
> are to be arranged so that they are both
> (a) reasonably expected to be to everyone's
> advantage, and (b) attached to positions and
> offices open to all.[45]

Rawls sometimes describes his position as a
theory of "Justice as Fairness." He means that
his two principles have to be regarded as fair
since they are precisely the principles any reasonable person behind the veil of ignorance would
adopt. The first principle is egalitarian. Every
person has an equal right to as much freedom as is
compatible for everyone else. The second principle states when deviations from the principle of
equal liberty are justified: namely, only in cases
when there is a reasonable expectation that those
inequalities will work to the advantage of everyone, and when the unequal positions and offices
are open to all.

Obviously, a 600 page book has a great deal
more to say about justice; but I have summarized
what seems to be the heart of his system. The
difficulties that arise from just these few

70

paragraphs are enough to cast doubt on the soundness of Rawls' approach. For one thing, Rawls never provides arguments to support his identification of the two principles of justice. His case rests on his confidence that reasonable readers will end up intuiting principles of justice identical with his own. This seems a rather shaky foundation for such a massive system. It is impossible to argue with someone whose position rests not on arguments, but on intuition.

Rawls repeatedly emphasizes the virtues of his veil of ignorance. His system is founded on the conviction that anyone in the original position who is subjected to the epistemological limitations of the veil of ignorance would select precisely his two principles. Brian Barry, one of Rawls' more astute critics, has observed that just because some principle of justice were adopted in a Rawlsian state of nature, it does not follow that the principle would be just. Barry asks us to imagine two men, one white and the other black, who find themselves in an original situation like Rawls describes. Behind the veil of ignorance, neither can know his own race. Suppose further, Barry continues, that in all other respects (ability, intelligence, training) the two men are equal. Imagine that they are given a choice between two situations. In the first, they both earn $100 a week. In the second, both would earn much more money. One of them would earn $1000 a week while the other earned $500 a week. Suppose they were told that the difference in salary would be based entirely on race, viz., the white man would earn twice as much as the black man. But the black man in the second situation would still earn five times as much as either man in the first situation. Barry reminds us that neither individual knows whether he will be the white or the black man. But whichever he is, he will earn at the very least five times more money. Which of the two situations would reasonable people opt for? Clearly, the second. But, Barry objects, this would result in reasonable people in a Rawlsian state of nature making a choice that is clearly unjust. It is unjust because the distribution is based solely on racial grounds. Therefore, Barry concludes, the principles that reasonable people would adopt in a Rawlsian original situation would not necessarily be just.[46]

Exception can also be taken to Rawls' principle that inequalities are justified only if they increase or do not decrease the advantages of the least advantaged members of society. John Hospers provides a damaging example:

> Suppose that the distribution of goods in a society (which for the sake of simplicity we shall take to consist of five persons only) is 6-6-4-4-4. Now an invention comes along which will enormously increase the standard of living, so that the resulting distribution becomes 50-50-40-40-3. Would it be justified? No, presumably the invention would have to be suppressed in spite of the great rise in the standard of living of almost everyone, because one person in the society is slightly worse off because of it.[47]

The example Hospers gives to complete his argument is the invention of the automobile. The introduction of the automobile provided thousands of new jobs, made millions happy because they could travel farther and faster at a reasonable cost. Everyone was better off "except the manufacturer of buggy-whips, who once did a land-office business but is now out of work because of the new invention."[48] Not even the money the former manufacturer of buggy-whips might receive on welfare can begin to compensate for what he lost by the invention of the automobile. No matter how much better off everyone else is, this one person has been disadvantaged. Would Rawls prohibit the invention? Since his second principle rules out inequalities that fail to work to the advantage of everyone, Hospers argues, "No major innovation would ever have occurred, from the dawn of history to the present, no matter how great its benefit to mankind," since there would always be "someone somewhere who [would be] worse off because of it."[49] It is manifest that Rawls' system requires major alterations.

RELIGIOUS APPEALS TO SOCIAL JUSTICE

One interesting feature of the current infatuation with statism is the affection with which it is held by many Christian clergymen. Friedrich Hayek is struck by the fact that much of the current interest in social justice occurs in clergymen "who, while increasingly losing their faith in a supernatural revelation, appear to have sought a refuge and consolation in a new 'social' religion which substitutes a temporal for a celestial promise of justice, and who hope that they can thus continue their striving to do good."[50] Several Christian organizations, for example, have in the name of social justice, made large donations to terrorist groups in Africa. Much less extreme is the position of a growing number of theologically conservative Protestants who insist that the Christian's undisputed obligation to demonstrate love for the needy is an integral part of justice. They believe that the Christian's social responsibility obliges him to adopt Liberal statist means to aid the poor. Some cast aspersions about the genuineness of a religious commitment that does not openly embrace a statist or Liberal approach to social justice. It is unlikely that all proponents of this position understand the extent to which their views enslave them to the State. It would not be the first time that Christians have made the mistake of encouraging the State to use its vast powers of coercion to help attain their ends. The spectre of the Inquisition is clearly visible, lurking in the background. No Christian should favor compulsion in bringing people to theological commitment. But is voluntarism any less essential to social virtue?

Such convictions clearly involve a confusion

of justice and love. By its very nature, the
State is an institution of coercion; it must operate through the use of force. Furthermore, if the
State is to appear just, it must operate impersonally. Not to act impersonally would be to discriminate among persons. Justice then can only be
effected through a State which uses force dispensed impersonally in accordance with law. But
this analysis of justice conflicts at every point
with the nature of love. Love, by definition,
must be given voluntarily; no one can be forced to
love. Moreover, love always discriminates; it is
always personal (directed at specific individuals).
And finally, love should be willing to sacrifice,
to go beyond the ordinary moral and legal requirements of a situation. A necessarily coercive
State cannot serve as an instrument of love. The
State's required use of force is logically incom-
patibile with the nature and demands of love. As
soon as the coercive State enters the picture,
love must leave. When the Christian statist confuses love with justice, he is doing more than
simply urging others in his society to manifest a
compassionate love for the needy. He is in effect
demanding that the State get out its weapons and
force people to fulfill the demands of love. And
how does the State do this? The State does this
by becoming an institutionalized Robin Hood. The
mythical Robin Hood is admired because he only
stole from thieves (agents of the State). The
Robin Hood State steals primarily from innocent
individuals whose only crime was some measure of
success or good fortune in life. Under statism,
giving is totally ignored. All emphasis is placed
on receiving, on who gets what. And, of course,
given the nature of statism, giving is supplanted
by taking, a taking effected by the State through
its powers of taxation.

In addition to the confusion between love and
justice, these modern attempts to support a statist approach to justice on religious grounds
involve a serious misreading of the Bible. Christian statists have convinced themselves that with
or without any support from economic and political

theory, the Bible commands a view of justice consistent with the values of political Liberalism. Because Scripture repeatedly mentions justice in contexts that also refer to love, to helping the poor, and to giving food to the hungry, it is not difficult for them to present a superficially plausible case for their position.[51] But these appeals to Scripture should be scrutinized very carefully. For example, some of the verses appealed to turn out to refer not to distributive justice but to remedial justice. This is clearly true in the case of Exodus 23:6 which warns against depriving the poor man of justice but makes it obvious that the justice referred to is that found in a court of law. The same chapter (23:3) also warns against showing partiality toward the poor in a court of law.

Most of the confusion present in these Christian attempts to find a theory of distributive justice in the Bible results from inattention to the classical distinction between a universal and a particular sense of justice, noted earlier in the chapter. Universal justice, it will be remembered, is co-extensive with the whole of righteousness, with the whole of virtue. Distributive justice, a species of particular justice, is something quite different. There is no reason to believe that any verse in the Bible conjoining justice with love or aid for the needy is an endorsement of any twentieth-century pattern of distributive justice. Since each verse like this[52] makes perfectly good sense as a reference to virtue or righteousness as a whole (i.e., justice in its universal sense), anyone who would make these verses say more must shoulder the burden of proof. The only way the Christian statist can begin to find his theory of social justice in Scripture is by confusing the biblical pronouncements about universal justice with his particular theory of distributive justice.[53] Because of the nature of universal justice, it is a simple matter to find justice conjoined in Scripture with love, charity, kindness to the poor, and help for the hungry. But it is logically irresponsible to infer from these statements that God endorses the welfare state, or Marxism (a claim made by advocates of Liberation Theology), or any other contemporary theory of distributive justice.

I have already declared my support for the view that a society with sufficient means should attempt to meet the needs of its citizens who cannot care for themselves. I have also argued that this has nothing to do with justice in its particular, distributive sense (social justice). If the Christian statist and I agree on the need to support the less fortunate, what difference does it make whether we call it justice or something else? It makes a great deal of difference, if the attempt to pack such notions into the concept of justice leads to conflicts with other social values, supports an expansion of statist powers, encourages an economic interventionism that makes it less likely that future generations will produce enough to take care of their needy, and results in social action that is counterproductive and actually harmful to the less fortunate members of society.

CONCLUSIONS

This long chapter has covered so much territory that a summary of the main conclusions we wish to assert may be helpful. (1) The word "justice" has several meanings ranging from its use as a synonym for righteousness to more particular usages in which people receive their due in commercial, remedial and distributive situations. (2) It has yet to be shown that the phrase "social justice" has any meaning. (3) Serious problems arise from any attempt to defend a pattern theory of justice. At the very least, such views are incompatible with a free society. (4) Justice is not based on forward-looking considerations; it clearly looks back to situational and personal factors relevant to what people are presently due. (5) Justice and equality are not the same. There are inequalities that are just and equalities

76

that are unjust. (6) Any confusion between love and justice should be avoided. (7) Likewise, the confusion between economic and moral merit can only lead to great mischief. (8) It seems best to avoid any suggestion that justice can be dealt with adequately in terms of any one overall pattern or principle. (9) Justice consists in giving people their due, that to which they have a right. As Brody writes,

> People have a variety of rights. They have these rights because of various factors of their past and present situation, their character and actions. They do not have them because of certain consequences of their having them. Different rights depend upon different factors. Justice consists in the satisfaction of these rights. This satisfaction results in certain equalities among people; they are the just equalities. It also results in certain inequalities among people; they are the just inequalities.[54]

And finally, (10) nothing in the nature of justice supports appeals to it as grounds for statism.

CHAPTER THREE

POLITICAL FREEDOM

The task of defining "freedom" is not easy.
Abraham Lincoln once observed, "The world has
never had a good definition of the word liberty,
and the American people just now are much in need
of one. We all declare for liberty; but in using
the same word, we do not mean the same thing."[1]
The meaning of this apparently simple word is
systematically elusive. "The word liberty means
nothing until it is given specific content, and
with a little massage it will take any content you
like."[2]

The quest for definitions of freedom and justice involves a high personal stake for everyone
involved. Unless great care is exercised, these
terms can be defined in ways that will make it
easier to justify state-induced injustices or
statist restraints upon individual liberty. Little effort is required to recall the many who have
been deprived of freedom and justice in the very
name of these values.

THE FOLLY OF ABSTRACT FREEDOM

An adequate notion of liberty must avoid the
folly of "Abstract Freedom." Edmund Burke, the
18th century British statesman, warned his coun-
trymen about the worship of the false goddess in
whose name so many crimes have been committed and
so many societies destroyed. This obsession with
abstract freedom was one of the major reasons for
the excesses of the French Revolution. Burke
asked, "Is it because liberty in the abstract may

be classed among the blessings of mankind, that I am seriously to felicitate a madman, who has escaped from the protecting restraint and wholesome darkness of his cell, on his restoration to the enjoyment of light and liberty? Am I to congratulate a highwayman and murderer, who has broken prison, upon the recovery of his natural rights?"[3] There is, Burke insisted, no such thing as freedom in the abstract. Only specific instances of liberty may be good or bad. James Fitzjames Stephen advanced the same claim a century after Burke:

> the question whether liberty is a good or bad thing appears as irrational as the question whether fire is a good or bad thing. It is both good and bad according to time, place and circumstances.... We must confine ourselves to such remarks as experience suggests about the advantages and disadvantages of compulsion and liberty in particular cases.[4]

Since abstract freedom does not exist, attention should be directed to the value or disvalue of specific instances of liberty.

THE FICTION OF ABSOLUTE FREEDOM

Many who speak in praise of liberty seem to be captivated by a dim vision of some kind of total or absolute freedom in which one can do anything he wants. But such an absolute freedom is a fiction, an unattainable ideal. No one can have or do whatever he wants at any time. All human beings and all human actions are limited by many different factors. First, every person's freedom is limited by the liberty of others. If one person were absolutely free, everyone else affected by his actions would have to be subservient to his wishes. Second, human freedom is also restricted by such things as circumstances, physical and intellectual limitations, and acts of God. Nature and society both place human beings under many restraints. If I'm to be free to breathe clean

air, someone else must be constrained not to pollute. If I'm to be free to live, others may need
to be coerced so as not to kill me. Total and
absolute freedom is a fiction that never has and
never will exist. Human beings can be free only
within certain limits.

THE MEANING OF FREEDOM

I propose, as a preliminary definition of
"freedom," to use the term in its classical sense,
the absence of coercion. While freedom may mean
more than this, it certainly cannot mean less.
Whatever the total scope of the term, it is clear
that deliberate restrictions on human choices and
actions by other human beings reduce or destroy
freedom. A person is free then to the extent that
he is not coerced or constrained by another person. When a person is subject to coercion, his
actions serve, not his own will, but the purpose
of someone else. "Freedom" is a relational term
that should be applied properly only to certain
relations between human beings, specifically those
relations not characterized by the presence of
coercion. The use of the word in contexts other
than those in which men are related to other men
(such as disclaiming freedom because one cannot
fly like a bird or because one lacks other powers
and abilities) can only result in confusion.

Much perplexity and turmoil has resulted from
the failure to keep freedom distinct from other
goods and values which may accompany it. For
example, many people feel their freedom is negated
when something they want or desire is kept from
them. The resulting feeling of frustration makes
it natural to suppose that freedom has something
to do with the satisfaction of wants and desires.
If a child wants a candy bar and is prevented from
getting one by a parent, the child's freedom has
been restricted and he feels frustration. But
does it follow from this that freedom and want-
satisfaction are identical? Clearly not, for it
is just as obvious that some constraints do not

result in frustration. Inversely, a person can be free without also being content. Freedom may or may not be productive of contentment. Therefore, even though the two values of freedom and satisfaction frequently accompany each other, they are not the same. They are distinct values that cannot be reduced to the other. Moreover, wants and desires can be the result of external coercion. A person can be conditioned to desire something. Equating liberty with satisfaction then would entail the silly view that any slave or prisoner could be freed by simply making him want to remain in his condition.

Nor are freedom and ability the same. It is one thing to ask if a person is free to do something; it is quite another to ask if he has the power to do it. Care should be taken not to confuse constraints with inabilities. Our understanding of freedom is not advanced by claiming that a person lacks freedom because he cannot (i.e., does not have the ability to) walk across the ocean. Some writers have insisted that political freedom unsupplemented by the power or ability to do something is a false freedom. For instance, a paraplegic might ridicule his alleged freedom of movement. But surely, as Feinberg comments, "our politically guaranteed liberty to move about at will is a genuine liberty and a genuine good, even though it may be worthless to a paralyzed person. What the invalid's plight shows is that health and mobility are also important and independent goods, not that political liberty is a sham."[5] Feinberg goes on to acknowledge

that a given person's lack of power or opportunity--his poverty, ignorance, or poor health--may be the indirect result of a structure of coercive laws.... Political liberty is best understood as the absence of political coercion...and not simply as de facto ability or opportunity. But where a law preventing a class of citizens from doing X leads indirectly to an absence of ability or opportunity for members of that class to

82

do Y, there is a clear reason to describe the latter as a negation of the liberty to do Y.[6]

Finally, freedom should not be confused with assorted social benefits like better housing and guaranteed income. While such benefits would make a person's freedom more valuable, they do not constitute freedom.

NEGATIVE AND POSITIVE FREEDOM

One common statist move to expand the power of the State involves an attempted redefinition of freedom in terms of positive freedom. The classical notion of liberty is disparaged as mere negative freedom. According to advocates of this alleged difference, negative freedom is freedom from some form of constraint or coercion while positive freedom is freedom to something. Negative freedom exists in the absence of external constraints deliberately imposed by other persons. Deliberate interference that prevents a person from doing something he would otherwise do is an abrogation of freedom in this negative sense. Positive freedom is supposed to consist in the power of a person to control his own affairs.

According to the usual statist apology for positive freedom, it does little good to be told that no one is preventing you from attaining some good while, all the time, you lack the power or the ability to satisfy your desires or attain your goal. It is not enough to be free from human interference or coercion. True freedom entails being able to achieve or to perform. Since the rich have more options than the poor, they thus have more freedom. Anyone sincerely interested in enhancing freedom should be willing to take steps to eliminate deficiencies like poverty and ignorance that deprive people of a greater range of choices. Something should be done to help people achieve positive freedom; the organization that can best accomplish this is the State. It should be obvious that the case for positive freedom will

83

result in a different assessment of statist action than a merely negative view. The person who is bewitched by a positive concept of liberty will believe that strong State action is necessary to overcome obstacles that stand in the way of being or doing or becoming something.

Several objections to the doctrine of positive freedom have been raised. For one thing, it is claimed, the doctrine is dangerous; it can lead to the tyranny of forcing people to be free. As Hayek warns,

> Once this identification of freedom with power is admitted, there is no end to the sophisms by which the attractions of the word 'liberty' can be used to support measures which destroy individual liberty, no end to the tricks by which people can be exhorted in the name of liberty to give up their liberty. It has been with the help of this equivocation that the notion of collective power over circumstances has been substituted for that of individual liberty and that in totalitarian states liberty has been suppressed in the name of liberty.[7]

Specious appeals to positive freedom can encourage people to think that deliberate restrictions on human choices that may appear to promote a public interest like welfare actually enhance liberty. This kind of thinking can easily lead to a situation where people no longer feel it necessary to justify certain coercive acts. When this stage is reached, can tyranny be far off?

Not only is the doctrine of positive freedom dangerous, it is also unclear. The apparent distinction between freedom from and freedom to is crude and simplistic. On more careful analysis, any significant differences between the two notions disappear, and the two kinds of freedom begin to blur into each other.[8] This can be seen in the case of a man locked in a prison cell. On the surface, the example appears to be a clear-

cut case of a violation of negative freedom, i.e.,
he lacks freedom from the bars and walls that con-
strain him. To be free, the prisoner must be free
from the bars that imprison him. His freedom is
restricted because of the presence of the bars.
But there is an alternative description of the
prisoner's situation. In the second account, the
man could be free if only he had a key to his
cell. His freedom is restricted because of the
absence of something, a key. While the first
account makes the prisoner's situation look like
an instance of negative freedom (or the absence of
it), the second description appears to be an
instance of positive freedom (or its absence).
The difference between the two accounts seems
trivial and hardly sufficient to support the distinction.

As another example, consider the case of a
man who is said to lack freedom because he never
received a certain kind of training. The absence
of this training or education could be interpreted by proponents of the two kinds of freedom
as a lack of positive freedom. If the training is
provided, then the man supposedly acquires the
freedom to do things he could not do before. Thus
he becomes free in the positive sense. But once
again, there is an alternative way of describing
the situation: the person's lack of training might
be explained as one result of the presence of certain conditions in the social system, e.g., racial
prejudice that prevents people of a particular
race from gaining the right kind of education. In
the alternate account, then, the alleged positive
freedom turns out to be indistinguishable from a
negative freedom.

Joel Feinberg believes the distinction
between negative and positive freedom rests on an
artificially limited idea of constraint.[9] As he
explains, the whole point to the alleged difference is that positive freedoms are not supposed to
contain any element of restraint. But once we
recognize the fact that people can be affected by
both external and internal restraints, the

distinction between the two kinds of freedom
breaks down. A man may be restrained from doing
something by different kinds of external restraint,
e.g., prison bars, a gun, or threat of physical
force. But people can also be restrained by
internal restraints, such as depression, illness,
or physical disability. From this it follows that
"there is no further need to speak of two distinct
kinds of freedom, one which has nothing to do with
constraint.... 'Freedom to' and 'freedom from'
are...logically linked, and there can be no special 'positive' freedom to which is not also a
freedom from."10 There thus seems to be no good
reason to continue distinguishing between negative
and positive freedom. This spurious move cannot
support any expansion of the minimal State.
Instead of talking about two kinds of freedom, it
appears to be better to think of but one kind of
freedom that is subject to two kinds of restraint,
internal and external.

Many philosophers, following Gerald MacCullum,
Jr.11 tend to regard statements of the form "X is
free" as abbreviations for longer expressions that
contain three elements. That is, every statement
about freedom implies a triadic relationship of
the form, "X is free from Y to do Z." Statements
about freedom specify who is free, what he is free
from, and what he is free to. The instantiations
of the variables X, Y, and Z will differ with the
context. Attempts to defend an exclusively positive sense of freedom do great injustice to the
total scope of liberty. Certainly the most
obvious element in any case of freedom is the
absence of direct, external compulsion or coercion. Freedom is the absence of coercion. While
freedom may be more than this, it certainly cannot
be less.12

THE PARADOX OF COERCION

The suggestion that political freedom is the
absence of coercion may appear to raise a puzzling
point that could be called the Paradox of

Coercion. Given that freedom requires the absence of coercion, it is also true that freedom cannot exist without coercion of some kind. It is impossible, in any human society, to eliminate all coercion. Every attempt to prevent some people from coercing others would itself be an act of coercion, or the threat of coercion. Since coercion can never be completely eliminated from human relationships, what should be strived for is a minimization of force or its harmful effects.

It is important to distinguish between force and violence. Violence is the use of force in an illegal or immoral way. It is true, of course, that one man's force is often another man's violence. That is, any act that some might view as a legitimate use of force could be viewed by others as violence. Force can be a good or evil depending on how it is used. The view that power itself is intrinsically evil is mistaken. Were any earthly society to abandon all use of force, it would simply create a power vacuum in which evil men would quickly gain control.

Political power is made necessary by the undeniable fact of human wickedness. Civil authorities must use force under law to discourage criminal disorder within society and aggression from without. According to St. Augustine, the purpose of the State is the maintenance of a peace on earth that will permit men to live in harmony and attain their rightful goals. This purpose is realized through the use of force and the fear of punishment. Should any human being find himself in a society not needing the apparatus of force (laws, courts, police, prisons) it is likely that he has entered the kingdom of God. The force used by earthly States is a necessary means in the restraint of evil men. Only as wicked men fear punishment will peace and security be possible. Force is needed to forestall violence, discourage criminals and other aggressors, encourage obedience to law, and attain social co-operation. The total elimination of force would effectively destroy whatever potential the State has for good, however little that might be.

Of course, the State also has potential for evil. This evil is realized most frequently either when the State fails to exercise the amount and kind of force required to prevent other evils such as crime; or when the State exercises too much force or the wrong kind of force. The use of force by the State must be limited to duly authorized institutions. If the State is necessary because of human evil, the State itself is a necessary evil since those who govern are sinful men. The possibility of power being abused is always present. Therefore there must be restraints and checks on the use of power. Augustine implied this when he taught that peace is always a kind of armistice between contending powers. As mentioned earlier, the American Founding Fathers recognized the dangers implicit in political power and developed a system of government in which power would be dispersed among several agencies of government, each of which would tend to check the others. The most important restraint on power is law. Force must be applied lawfully and without caprice or discrimination. Law is needed to prevent the indiscriminate or the selective use of force against a few for no lawful reason. Law without force is impotent; but force without law is blind. Force is, in a sense, the other side of the coin we call law. It is implicit in all law as a latent sanction.

FREEDOM AND THE RULE OF LAW

Every person's ultimate protection against coercion requires his control over some private spheres where he can be free. The theory of natural rights identifies one such sphere; private property is another. One of the most important limitations of governmental power is The Rule of Law. As John Locke wrote in his Second Treatise of Civil Government:

The end of law is not to abolish or
restrain, but to preserve and enlarge freedom. For in all the states of created
beings, capable of laws, where there is no
law there is no freedom. For liberty is to
be free from restraint and violence from
others, which cannot be where there is no
law, and is, as we are told, 'a liberty for
every man to do what he lists.'[13]

The Rule of Law is found whenever the agents
and arbiters in a situation are bound in advance
by fixed and stated rules or laws. Within the
limits of the rules, men are free to act to the
best of their ability. Of course, some play the
game better than others and are rewarded more
lucratively. Our freedoms come into conflict with
the liberties of others and with the limitations
of our circumstances and abilities. In order to
preserve order admidst these conflicting claims,
the State is given the monopoly of coercive power
within its sphere of control. But it is vital in
a free society that the power of the State be limited to laws which the citizen knows in advance.
When the actions of the government are not
announced in advance in the form of laws, it is
impossible for the citizen to predict what the
government will do or demand in any given situation. Thus the citizen's liberty is restricted
because he cannot plan his own future actions,
given his uncertainty about what the State will
approve or condemn the next hour, day, or week.
Where governments observe the Rule of Law, individuals can predict how the State will use its
coercive powers in given circumstances and can
thus govern their lives in a manner that will
enable them to avoid penalties for improper conduct. Once the individual knows the rules of the
game, he is free to pursue his personal ends so
long as they do not conflict with the pre-
announced rules. The Rule of Law prevents the
State from taking ad hoc, arbitrary, and discriminatory action. Obviously, the Rule of Law is a
necessary but not a sufficient condition for
liberty. Unjust laws could also deprive citizens

of important liberties.

While the Liberal statist may profess concern for the Rule of Law, he persists in taking actions that are not only inconsistent with the rule but also destructive of it. In the real world, natural inequalities exist. Driven by egalitarian concerns, the Liberal statist wants to overcome these natural differences. But this means that in his desire to make unequal people equal, he must treat them unequally. He must apply the rules in some cases and not in others. Or else he must have one set of rules for the people he identifies as disadvantaged and another set of rules for the rest.

FREEDOM AND HUMAN RIGHTS

Representatives of several different political traditions maintain the necessary interdependence of human freedom and natural rights. The contemporary Libertarian, Murray Rothbard, asserts: "Freedom is a condition in which a person's ownership rights in his own body and his legitimate material property are _not_ invaded, are not aggressed against. A man who steals another man's property is invading and restricting the victim's freedom, as does the man who beats another over the head."[14] The claim of the Conservative, Frank Meyer, that freedom is grounded in the nature of man and the constitution of being implies a close tie between liberty and natural rights. As Meyer wrote, "The rights of human beings...are not the gift of some Leviathan; they are inherently derived from the nature of men. The duties of human beings are not tribute owed to Leviathan; they are moral imperatives grounded in objective value."[15] Robert Nozick affirms that the only justification for the State is its role as servant and protector of natural human rights, a function that can be provided quite adequately by a minimal State. But when the State's power expands, the State itself becomes a trespasser against the very rights it is supposed to protect. _That_ State must

90

be condemned and resisted. In other words, "A minimal state, limited to the narrow functions of protection against force, theft, fraud, enforcement of contracts, and so on, is justified.... any more extensive state will violate a person's rights not to be forced to do certain things, and is unjustified."16

Many statements about human rights have been made in the past two hundred years. The American Declaration of Independence declared that "all men are created equal, that they are endowed by their Creator with certain inalienable Rights, that among these are Life, Liberty, and the pursuit of Happiness." Similar notions of inherent human rights have been central in much modern thinking about man's relationship to others and the State.

Natural rights are rights that men possess regardless of the decrees and policies of a State. Natural rights are grounded on the law of God and on human dignity, a dignity that, in my view, man possesses by virtue of his creation in the image of God. Positive rights, on the other hand, are given by the State, grounded on positive law and backed by some sanction. Foes of natural rights protest that it is foolish to talk about natural rights that are not recognized by the State, that are not expressed in positive rights. Well, it certainly helps when the rights recognized by the State accord with a human being's natural rights. But Legal Positivism effectively strips citizens of an appeal to any rights which a State refuses to recognize. As Leo Strauss observed, "To reject natural right is tantamount to saying that all right is positive right, and this means that which is right is determined exclusively by the legislators and the courts of the various countries."17 Strauss is surely correct. Unqualified Positivism entails that positive law can never be judged in terms of its conformity to a higher Moral Law, the law of God.

To have a right is to have a legally or morally justifiable claim to possess or obtain something or to act in a certain way. Having a right is a triadic relationship involving the person possessing the right, other persons having a duty to observe that right, and the object or thing which the right concerns. In many cases (those that philosophers call "Demand Rights"), rights and duties are correlative. That is, if A has a right with respect to B, then B has a corresponding duty with respect to A. Every demand right then is simply a duty looked at from a different perspective. Therefore certain claims that at one time are stated in terms of rights can at other times be expressed in terms of duties. Thus the second table of the Decalogue can be viewed not only as a list of man's duties to other human beings, but also as a list of human rights. It seems best not to regard any human rights as absolute or inalienable. Human rights frequently come into conflict and require adjudication. Even the Bible recognizes that the human right to life can be surrendered for a capital offense.

The state of rights found in the Declaration of Independence differs from the two other major statements in at least one significant way. Unlike the French Declaration of the Rights of Man (1789) and the Universal Declaration of Human Rights adopted by the United Nations General Assembly in 1948, the Declaration of Independence clearly related human rights to man's creaturely relationship to God. Whereas the United Nations statement simply avoids reference to any transcendent and divine ground of human rights, the French Declaration was openly hostile to theistic presuppositions. The French philosophes of the eighteenth century, rejecting the view that man is essentially evil and unable to redeem himself or society, developed a doctrine of the rights of man in conscious opposition to the Christian view of man. Then as today, humanism erred in regarding human rights as ends in themselves divorced from any reference to God.

One of the major tasks of any theory of natural rights is the discovery of an adequate ground for those rights. Regrettably, it is much easier to affirm the existence of natural rights than it is to defend the claim. The definitive philosophical defense of a natural rights position has yet to be written. Skepticism that any adequate Naturalistic ground will ever be found seems justified. I believe the quest for any adequate ground of natural rights must go beyond the speculations of Aristotelian metaphysics or Kantian anthropology. My own view is that God is the source and sanction of human rights, that human rights are a means to the end of aiding men in meeting their duties to God, and that government exists for the primary purpose of protecting basic human rights. Unfortunately, I know of no philosophical argument that will prove these contentions. One virtue of my position is that the presupposition of God as the ground of human rights avoids the Naturalist's inability to explain why human beings have a value, a dignity, and rights not possessed by dogs, fish, or camels. I suspect that the most that any philosopher qua philosopher can do is point out the totalitarian implications of any denial of natural rights. The limitation of the scope of individual rights exclusively to positive rights makes human beings subject to the whims and caprice of dictatorial States.

G. K. Chesterton once suggested that all men might be equal in the same way that all British pennies are equal. Some pennies are brighter than others just as some men are brighter. But every penny has the same value as any other penny because it is stamped with the image of the King. Similarly, Chesterton argued, however men may differ in external or non-essential respects, all are equal since they bear the image of the King of Kings. Many philosophers, no doubt, feel discomfort in the presence of language like this. Ironically, many attempts to provide a purely philosophic defense of natural rights amount to much the same thing. For example, L. T. Hobhouse once wrote,

As a matter of the interpretation of experience, there is something peculiar to human beings and common to human beings without distinction of class, race or sex, which lies far deeper than all differences between them. Call it what we may, soul, reason, the abysmal capacity for suffering, or just human nature, it is something generic, of which there may be many specific, as well as quantitative differences, but which underlies and embraces them all. If this common nature is what the doctrine of equal rights postulates, it has no reason to fear the test of our ordinary experience of life, or of our study of history and anthropology.[18]

While I do not believe that Hobhouse's doctrine of metaphysical equality can be defended by considerations that are exclusively philosophical, something like it occupies an important place in the Christian view of man. Man is made in God's image; all human beings are carriers of the image of God. Human rights are grounded in the very being of man as a creature of God. While the philosopher, Joel Feinberg, might not appreciate his position juxtaposed with such theological comments, he speaks for many when he writes:

> It seems evident to most of us that merely being human entitles everyone--bad men as well as good, lazy as well as industrious, inept as well as skilled--to a fair trial if charged with a crime, to equal protection of the law, to equal consideration of his interests by makers of national policy, to be spared torture or other cruel and inhuman treatment, and to be permanently ineligible for the status of chattel slave.[19]

The convictions Feinberg articulates might be nothing but an irrational prejudice; on the other hand, they might well be grounded on man's creaturely relation to God, or on some as yet undiscovered argument.

Many advocates of natural rights, including more than a few libertarians, follow the erroneous

94

lead of Thomas Paine's Rights of Man and the
French Declaration, and confuse human rights with
human wants. This confusion is found, for example, in the United Nations Declaration. Such
alleged rights as the right to equal pay, the
right to marry, the right to enjoy the arts, and
even the right to be idle, are more aspirations
than rights. If the right to marry really were a
demand right, it would follow that for every man
in the world, some woman would have the duty to
marry him. The implications of such a suggestion,
given the character and dispositions of many men,
would be so inhumane to the poor women involved as
to disqualify the natural rights doctrine as a
moral theory.

CONCLUSION

Our exploration of the concept of liberty has
found no reasons that justify any State greater
than the minimal State. No good reason has been
found for modifying the classical notion of liberty as the absence of coercion. Attempts to go
beyond the classical notion and define freedom in
terms of ability or want-satisfaction result only
in serious confusions. The appeal to a so-called
positive notion of freedom is both dangerous and
untenable. Even though the preservation of human
freedom requires that the State be given the power
to enforce the law, the State must not abuse its
power by aggressing against basic human rights.

CHAPTER FOUR

FREEDOM, MORALITY AND THE LAW

FREEDOM AND VIRTUE

To a great extent, the 19th century struggle
between conservative social thought and classical
liberalism was a conflict between those tradition-
alists who stressed objective values and order,
and the liberals who emphasized freedom and the
importance of the individual. Surprisingly, a
great many contemporary social theorists still
cling to the dichotomy of freedom and virtue.
Many who believe that the preservation of social
order requires the observance of unchanging moral
laws tend to view any emphasis on liberty as a
threat. Many friends of freedom see any defense
of moral order as an equally grave threat to their
cause.

Nineteenth century conservative thought
deserves both praise and blame, praise for its
clear affirmation that no society can survive if
it repudiates the objective moral laws that provide the structure of social order, and blame for
its frequent indifference to the cause of liberty.
The situation was reversed in nineteenth century
liberalism. While liberalism's commitment to
freedom was admirable, its defense of liberty was
inadequate. Most nineteenth century liberals
tried to defend freedom on utilitarian grounds,
which meant that the case for liberty depended
entirely on freedom producing consequences of a
certain kind, e.g., happiness for the greatest
number of people. The utilitarian defense of liberty was weak since it would only work for those
who shared the liberal's preferences for the ends

of individual human beings over the ends of society. Grounding the case for liberty on nothing more substantial than human preference left open the possibility that utilitarians could disavow freedom should they become persuaded that their preferred ends could be attained more successfully through coercive measures. In fact, this was precisely the direction taken by the thought of John Stuart Mill. As Frank Meyer urged, there must be a stronger case for freedom.

> Freedom as an essential right of men is founded not upon preferences, but upon the nature of men and the very constitution of being. [Freedom] is inalienable and infeasible as a right, not for any reasons of utility but because it is the true condition of man's created being. In the argument with collectivism, utilitarian reason can always be answered with alternative utilitarian reasons. The final struggle with collectivism ...can only be waged in terms of an understanding with the nature of man.[1]

Meyer's own position on the alleged dichotomy between freedom and order is instructive. Meyer came to see that freedom should not be viewed simply as a means to preferred ends. He believed that freedom must be grounded on a Christian view of being and man. Man's essential freedom and his right to exercise that freedom are his by virtue of his creation in God's image. To be truly human, to be most expressive of all the potential that being a carrier of the divine image implies, requires that human beings be free; they must be able to choose. When the State deprives man of his liberty, man loses an essential part of his humanness.

As noted, the first error of nineteenth century liberalism was its failure to ground man's freedom in the nature of man's created being. The classical liberal's second mistake was the fear of acknowledging an objective and transcendent ground of value. Because utilitarianism was incompatible with unchanging moral ends, classical liberalism lacked an "ultimate sanction for the inviolability of the person" and was left without any foundation for "its defense of the person as primary in political and social matters."[2] As M. Stanton Evans observes, "If there is no value system with which we may rebuke the pretensions of despots, what is to prevent the rule of force in the world? If there are no objective standards of right and wrong, why object to tyranny?"[3] According to Meyer,

> The Christian understanding of the nature and destiny of man, which is the foundation of Western civilization, is always and everywhere what conservatives strive to conserve. That understanding accepts the existence of absolute truth and good and at the same time recognizes that men are created with the free will to accept or reject that truth and good. Conservatism, therefore, demands both the struggle to vindicate truth and good and the establishment of conditions in which the free will of individual persons can be effectively exercised.[4]

Meyer's use of the conservative label to identify his position may puzzle readers inclined to equate conservatism with the authoritarian traditionalism of the nineteenth century conservatives or with the twentieth century disciples of Edmund Burke.[5] In the view of Meyer and many others, contemporary American conservatism should not be confused with nineteenth century traditionalism. He believed that there is a center, a consensus, a mainstream of conservatism in America that is, in fact, a fusion of two streams of thought: the classical liberal's respect for the liberty of the individual person and the traditional conservative's respect for objective and unchanging moral values. As Meyer wrote,

> I believe that those two streams of thought, although they are sometimes presented as mutually incompatible, can in reality be

united within a single broad conservative political theory, since they have their roots in a common tradition and are arrayed against a common enemy.[6]

Moreover, conservatives like Meyer believe their fusion of libertarianism and traditionalist concerns faithfully reflects the view of the Founding Fathers. Conservatives believe that the Constitution's program of protecting individual freedom in an ordered society governed by a limited State "was the closest that human beings have come to establishing a polity which gives the possibility of maintaining at one and the same time individual liberty, underlying norms of law, and necessary public order."[7] In another book, Meyer drew the following conclusions:

> The American conservative has indeed a special heritage, the discussions and the achievements of the Founders of the American Constitution (Madison preeminently), men who established the highest political form the West has yet created to express the tension of transcendent truth and human freedom. The political structure they left us has its contradictions, no doubt; but...they reflect the imperfect state of man and the tension within which he must live if he is to be true to his nature, striving towards transcendent ends in freedom.[8]

The claim that America has a political tradition, grounded in the Founding Fathers, that preserves the virtues and avoids the excesses both of classic libertarianism and continental authoritarianism should be interesting news to anyone who recognizes society's need for both freedom and virtue. Unfortunately, the tendency to exalt either freedom or virtue at the expense of the other is still prevalent in contemporary political thought. One common manifestation of this dichotomy is the insistence that freedom should be viewed only as a means to certain ends, in this case, virtuous actions. Consequently, this view maintains, freedom that is not used to achieve the right ends is not true freedom. Meyer objected to any attempt to present virtue and freedom as mutually exclusive alternatives. For Meyer, virtue without freedom is impossible and freedom without virtue is empty. Instead of thinking freedom or virtue, we should think freedom and virtue. The two are not contradictories. No society lacking either condition can be a good society.

The reason why virtue without freedom is impossible is simple. It is logically impossible to force a person to be virtuous. Even though acts of a certain type may be virtuous, no one who performs those acts against his will can be virtuous. Freedom is a condition of both virtue and vice. But whether a particular person's freedom leads to virtue or vice, the freedom itself is an indispensable condition to either state. The elimination of freedom can never enhance virtue; its elimination can only make the attainment of virtue impossible.

What did Meyer mean by the claim that freedom without virtue is empty? He argued that even though freedom is a necessary condition for anyone's living a virtuous life, freedom by itself lacks both content and purpose if divorced from "an objective moral order which men should strive to understand and move towards."9

Up to this point, Meyer's refusal to disjoin freedom and virtue strikes me as admirable. From here, however, things begin to get sticky. As Meyer continued the development of his own position, it becomes apparent that freedom and virtue became unglued in his own theory. Meyer went on to contend that freedom and virtue belong to entirely separate realms. Virtue belongs to the intellectual, moral and spiritual order (the individual), while freedom belongs to the political order (the State). As if this move were not debatable enough, Meyer insisted on removing virtue from the social sphere as well. I believe Meyer was trapped into a betrayal of his own

101

program of conjoining freedom and virtue by an unresolved tension in his theory. Once a commitment is made to what chapter one called radical anti-statism, it is difficult to see how one can consistently avoid a social atomism that is basically incompatible with community. Meyer's difficulties, along with a more satisfactory approach to the question of freedom and virtue, will be charted in the next section.

MORAL MAN AND MORAL SOCIETY

Meyer offered one basic reason why he did not believe society should be given a role in the determination of virtue: he thought it would lead to despotism. Once society is given any rights over the individual, he thought, the inevitable result must be tyranny. He wrote, "community conceived as a principle of social order prior and superior to the individual person, can justify any oppression of individual persons so long as it is carried out in the name of 'community,' of society or of its agent, the state. This is the principle of collectivism."10

Meyer's reasoning is anything but clear. The discussion of anarchism in chapter one showed how even anarchists can recognize that an emphasis on community can be compatible with radical anti-statism. In fact, it is voluntary associations that provide the anarchist with his grounds for social order. Thus, while anarchists like Rothbard believe that voluntary associations can replace the police, armies and judges of existing States, Meyer seemed to see a threat in any coalition of two or more people. Meyer confused his reader even more with assurances that his anti-social type of individualism was not a form of social atomism, by which he meant the view that "the person is a monad-like atom, cut off and isolated from other persons."11 Meyer's disavowal of social atomism was buttressed with frequent praise for the role that human interrelationships play in the development of the individual person.

102

But could Meyer have it both ways? How can any view that rejects social atomism and then rejects community possibly be consistent? Meyer rejected the dilemma that would force the defender of liberty to choose between the priority of community over the individual person or the repudiation of love, friendship, and community. He wrote,

> The dilemma is false: only individual persons, conscious each in his own uniqueness, can reach out and establish relations with other persons, relations charged with the content, vibrant with the tone, that all of us know unmistakably on the basis of our direct awareness. To assert the freedom and independence of the individual person implies no denial of the value of mutuality, of association and common action between persons. It only denies the value of coerced association.[12]

In several respects, this is an impressive paragraph. But the merits of what Meyer was attempting to say should not blind us to his oversimplification. The kind of coercion one finds in voluntary associations is quantitatively and qualitatively different from the use of force exercised by the State. To claim, as Meyer did, that an individual's voluntary submission to the limited coercion of a society must lead inevitably to the monopolistic use of force practiced by the State requires support not found anywhere in Meyer's writings. My point here will be developed shortly as the first of four objections to Meyer's position. Before those arguments are presented, however, it will prove useful to examine the alternative approach of Robert Nisbet.

According to Nisbet, when individual persons cease to be held together in communities, they become so atomized, isolated, and alienated that they become easy prey for an expansionist political power. Thus, while Meyer saw the emphasis on society as entailing tyranny, Nisbet sees the isolation of the individual from society as supporting despotism. Nisbet's moderate anti-statism opposes the kind of State that deifies unity and destroys social diversity. Nisbet rejects any unification of human relationships under the aegis of the State by defending a pluralism of voluntary communities. Instead of placing all of his bets on the State, Nisbet prefers a plurality of societies based on location, occupation, belief, class, and other non-coercive ties. Even Meyer approved of Nisbet's position to a point when he wrote:

> Better a multitude of enforced collectivities, so that the individual human being may wrest for himself an area of autonomy out of simultaneous partial loyalty to several of them, or out of precarious existence in the interstices between them, than a single all-embracing Leviathan community which will totally subordinate him.[13]

This modest praise aside, Meyer objected to Nisbet's position on the ground that Nisbet was simply replacing the impersonal and brutal tyranny of the totalitarian State with the "subtler, quiet tyranny of 'customarily' imposed community, in which no one can escape from the deadly environment of hereditarily or geographically imposed association."[14] One must pause and reflect on the fairness of Meyer's description of human membership in a society as a "mild form of tyranny." Only if one stacks the deck in this way does it become necessary to seek what Meyer called his third way. Only this kind of question-begging would seem to make necessary Meyer's own strained attempts to assign freedom and virtue to entirely different spheres.

I believe Meyer's position is unsatisfactory for at least four reasons. (1) Meyer surely exaggerated when he described Nisbet's view of society as a more subtle tyranny which leads inescapably to the brutal tyranny of totalitarianism. A simple example may help make my point clear. The National Football League is, without question, a

voluntary association. Like any society, the NFL
has rules that govern players and management, both
on and off the football field. Unnecessary roughness during a game results in a fifteen yard pen-
alty; unnecessary roughness after a game would
result in more serious sanctions. Association
with known gamblers could lead to expulsion from
the sport. As a society, then, the NFL has a set
of rules that are analogous to a kind of public
morality, at least a "morality" binding on every
member of the society. When any individual
chooses to become a part of the association, he
surrenders some of his right to dissent with
regard to the rules. The game could not be played
if the participants were free to ignore the rules
whenever they liked. Imagine a situation on the
fifty yard line during a game where a 280 pound
defensive end registers his disapproval of a pen-
alty by beating the official to a pulp. Meyer
would have us believe that any submission to the
rules of a football league or church or lodge or
union is the first step toward tyranny. Surely,
this is unwarranted. The analogy also allows us
to see how certain violations of a society's rules
might be so serious as to require punishment under
civil or criminal law. For example, a particular
instance of unnecessary roughness might be so
vicious as to subject the perpetrator to criminal
charges.

(2) Meyer's second error was to confuse two
entirely different ways in which force and virtue
can be related. Many libertarians ask if force
can advance morality and assume a negative answer.
They disappoint by asking a complex question and
expecting a simple answer. The question, can
force advance morality, may be taken in two quite
different senses that require two quite different
responses: (1) can people be made virtuous by
forcing them to behave in certain ways? (2) Can
the moral tone of a society be improved or maintained by enforcing some standards of conduct?

The late British philosopher, Sir David Ross,
offered a distinction between _morally_ _good_ actions

105

and right acts that helps to clarify our point.15
Ross made his distinction in order to draw attention to the fact that any moral behavior can be
viewed from at least two perspectives: (1) from
the outer perspective, the agent's overt act, one
can ask if the person's behavior was fitting, if
it was the right thing to do; (2) from the inner
perspective, one can ask if the behavior was morally good, i.e., if the agent's motives or intentions were good?

The rightness of an act, according to Ross,
has nothing to do with the agent's reasons for
doing it. Any act's rightness is determined
solely by whether it was or was not the correct,
the fitting, the proper thing to do in that case.
To help a little old lady across the street is the
right thing to do, providing of course that she
wishes to cross the street. But obviously, people
can do all sorts of right acts for the wrong reasons. For example, one's motive for assisting the
lady might be a selfish desire for reward. This
possibility led Ross to the second part of his
distinction, morally good actions. An action is
morally good if the agent's motives are good.
With this distinction before us, let us return to
the libertarian's question, can force advance morality?

Meyer's claim that people cannot be forced to
behave virtuously obviously had morally good
actions in view. Since an action cannot possibly
be morally good unless the agent's intentions are
virtuous and unless he acts freely, Meyer's thesis
is logically true. But Meyer overlooked the fact
that there may be other reasons why people might
have to be forced, viz., to perform right acts.
The well-being of individuals and the preservation
of social order usually depends upon people doing
the right thing, whether they want to or not.
Individuals and society would experience some difficulty if they had to wait for rapists, embezzlers, strong-arm men, and the like to acquire a
virtuous character and start performing morally
good actions. Without doubt, it would be

106

preferable that people do the right thing (e.g., tell the truth, refrain from stealing) from a fixed and settled virtuous disposition. But given the flawed character of human nature and the subsequent improbability that such a state of affairs will ever exist to any great degree, it is at least preferable that people do the right thing regarding certain minimal standards of conduct, even when forced to by the law. For good or ill, the threat of force can help persuade many otherwise undecided moral agents that they had best refrain from certain acts, even if their behavior does not reflect the wishes of their heart.

(3) Meyer's third mistake was his oversimplification of the relationship between the individual and society. Meyer's individual was related to society only because he, the individual, chose to be.[16] Meyer gave little evidence that he recognized that no human being can be isolated from society without it affecting his humanness. The recognition by Aristotle and Aquinas that man is a social animal is a more adequate account of the relation between individuals and society. In the words of Aquinas,

> It must be understood that, because man is by nature a social animal, needing many things to live which he cannot get for himself if alone, he naturally is a part of a group that furnishes him help to live well. He needs this help for two reasons. First, to have what is necessary for life, without which he cannot live the present life; and for this, man is indebted to his parents for his generation and his nourishment and instruction. Likewise, individuals, who are members of the family, help one another to procure the necessities of life. In another way, man receives help from the group of which he is a part, to have a perfect sufficiency for life; namely, that man may not only live but live well, having everything sufficient for living; and in this way man is helped by the civic group, of which he is a

107

member, not only in regard to bodily needs...
but also in regard to right conduct, inasmuch
as public authority restrains with fear of
punishment delinquent young men whom paternal
admonition is not able to correct.17

The young, immature human being is dependent on
the society of others for his very life and training. The adult, mature human requires the society
of others in order to live a fully human life.

Even the anti-statist, Friedrich Hayek,
appears to contradict Meyer's extreme individualism when he acknowledges that a True Individualism
"affirms the value of the family and all the common efforts of the small community and group...
[and] believes in local autonomy and voluntary
associations...indeed its case rests largely on
the contention that much for which the coercive
action of the state is usually invoked can be
done better by voluntary collaboration...."18 It
is a False Individualism, Hayek continues, "which
wants to dissolve all these smaller groups [i.e.,
societies] into atoms which have no cohesion other
than the coercive rules imposed by the state...."19
Meyer erred then by undervaluing the extent to
which human society provides human beings with the
occasions for developing their most essential
human traits. Even though we are individuals, we
are individuals bound necessarily to community.
Thus, we cannot help but be concerned about the
characteristics of those societies, including
their morality.

(4) Meyer's fourth error was exaggerating the
extent to which the individual alone, apart from
society, is the primary locus of virtue. Meyer
left his reader with the impression that the
values of individual people are attained in isolation from their society. He apparently failed to
appreciate the extent to which the individual's
values are shaped by his social and moral environment. Society may either aid or hinder the development of virtue. As William Lillie put it, "the
life of society is the normal atmosphere, and

indeed the training ground of morality. Our moral
ideas develop in association with those of other
people and are being constantly criticized and
modified by the opinions of others.... There may
be exceptional cases like those of the saint or
the ascetic where the individual finds his station
and its duties away from society, but for the
normal man morality is a social business."20
Society is indeed the "background of the moral
life."21 Of course, nothing we have said implies
that the social dimension of morality should be
exaggerated to the point that the individual
becomes subordinate to the larger group. This
could easily lead to the destruction of essential
moral concerns. But Meyer's fear that granting
society any voice in morality opens the door to
despotism is ungrounded. The locus of virtue has
two poles. Meyer was wrong in advancing the disjunction, either the individual or society. Such
a disjunction makes the realization of Meyer's own
program of virtue and freedom unattainable. Those
who follow Meyer's lead of assigning virtue and
freedom to incompatible spheres will find themselves forced to choose virtue or freedom. When
the relationship between the individual and society is properly understood, Meyer's ideal of virtue and freedom is attainable.

MORALITY AND SOCIETY

The relationship of society to morality has
three aspects. It can be argued that a legitimate
function of society is: (1) the formation of character; or (2) the enforcement of a public morality, the common set of beliefs and values which
bind the members of the society together; or
(3) the enforcement of those minimal standards of
conduct which are absolutely essential for the
survival of society.

When society is viewed as the smaller social
units such as a family, church or club we are all
a part of, any of these functions is easily
affirmed. But many people get uncomfortable when

these moral roles are assigned to society as a whole. There is an inconsistency of attitudes toward the recognizable moral function of a small social unit and the alleged moral function of society as a whole. At what point in the expanding circle of societal relationships does the moral function cease to be proper? At what point does it become dangerous in the sense of threatening liberty? These difficult questions must be by-passed while the three possible relationships between society and morality are examined in more detail.

1. <u>The formation of character is a legitimate concern and function of society</u>. It is difficult to imagine a society that is unconcerned with the conduct and character of its members. Even the Mafia has a code. Most societies play a pivotal role in civilizing their members. There seems to be little reason to question the legitimacy of this function when performed by social units like the family or the church.

Problems multiply, however, when this principle is extended to suggest that the formation of character is a legitimate concern of the State. One philosopher who held this view was Aristotle. He wrote that "Lawgivers make the citizens good by training them in habits of right action--this is the aim of all legislation, and if it fails to do this it is a failure; this is what distinguishes a good form of constitution from a bad one."[22] A contemporary advocate of Aristotle's position, Walter Berns, holds that "the formation of character is the principal duty of government."[23] According to another proponent, L. Brent Bozell, a society must choose between two mutually exclusive goals--either the maximization of freedom or the maximization of virtue.[24] Bozell does not believe that any society can consistently strive toward both goals at the same time. Bozell believes that any individual committed to an objective moral code must regard it as his duty to use the apparatus of the State to promote those truths.

110

As I indicated, the right of the smaller
social units to influence the moral beliefs, character and conduct of their members seems indisputable. Concern about the legitimacy of the
function seems to increase in proportion to the
size, influence, and power of the society. It
would be difficult to find much wide-spread
approval of Aristotle's position in liberal Western societies. The major objection is obvious:
how does one guarantee that the people who make
the laws are training citizens in the correct
moral beliefs? What is to prevent a State with
such powers from declaring one's own cherished
beliefs to be obscene or immoral? This is not to
say that any State can be or should be unconcerned
with the morality of its citizens; it is only to
recognize the dangers involved in granting to the
State functions that belong to society. In spite
of the problems of this theory, it does contain a
moment of truth. Harry Clor explains that the
position could be interpreted so that the civilizing function of the law is not performed simply
by preventing or punishing crime. Understood in
this way, "The negative or coercive role of law
is, ultimately, subordinate to its positive or
educative role. Legislation seeks not merely to
prevent the worst evils, but also to promote such
higher forms of conduct and character as will
serve the higher purposes of the community."25

     2. Societies have the right to enforce the
common set of beliefs and values which bind their
members together. "A society functions only if
its members share a common body of values, and
back of it, a common ethos. This permits some
divergencies but also requires the society, if it
is to remain viable, to protect the essential
shared values."26 Every society has some kind of
shared or public morality and has the right to be
concerned about the preservation of its beliefs
and values. Few societies could survive a widely
held disregard for the values of honesty and
truth-telling. A church, for example, can decide
which beliefs and standards it expects its members
to maintain; it can also exlude those members who

111

reject its code.

At least two problems arise when this function is extended to the State. First, how does the State know if the public morality is true? How does the State know with certainty what the public morality is? Failure to answer either question adequately would sink the second theory.

To summarize the discussion of the first two theses, smaller social units appear to have legitimate concern with the moral character of their members and their observance of that society's "public morality." Opposition to these principles within a free society increases as the moral training or enforcement is extended to increasingly larger circles of community, and finally to the State. Many oppose the use of the law to form character or enforce a particular morality. But these objections should not blind us to the fact that each of the first two theories does contain moments of truth, even for the most general levels of society. As Clor asks, "If citizens are taught that the promotion of good character is no function whatever of the political community, how are they likely to be affected by laws designed to prevent the grosser forms of moral debasement?"[27] Moreover, he continues,

> the significance of common values--of a moral consensus--must be recognized even in a liberal society. Communal life, at least decent communal life, requires mutual trust and respect. And it is a requisite for mutual trust and respect that certain fundamental attitudes and beliefs be held in common. No large body of men can be continuously bound together on the sole basis of the principle that values are a matter of personal choice.... If decent social life requires that men believe something together, what they believe together must include a body of substantive values which are thought sufficiently important to warrant (at times) their imposition at the expense of dissent.[28]

112

Clor's comments provide some helpful balance to the discussion. With respect to morality, society, and the State, it is easy to err with respect to either extreme. Perhaps the third thesis will provide a more satisfactory resolution of our problems.

3. Societies have the right to enforce minimal standards of conduct which are absolutely indispensable for their survival. Some social philosophers believe this thesis is the most promising one on which to develop a relationship between society and morality. Whether or not the issue of a public morality should be pushed, it seems obvious that there are minimal standards of conduct, the violation of which can destroy any society. If enough members of a society fall victim to a particular vice (or set of vices), the society may become so weak that it cannot stand up to serious challenges.

> According to the argument now under consideration, the law is concerned with such morality as a precondition for the willingness or capacity of men to contribute to the common tasks and interests of a community. The law is obliged to set such standards as will deter any large number of citizens from sinking below this level of morality.... If these requisites are not met and the duties are improperly performed or not performed, then social life is debased and the form of government is endangered. Government may concern itself with morality, not in order to promote the virtuous character of individuals, but in order to prevent such a degree of vice as is incompatible with the health of society and the security of government.[29]

Lord Devlin's well-known book, The Enforcement of Morals, among other arguments, grounds its case for the enforcement of morality on this principle. Devlin recognized that this type of appeal is not based on paternalistic concerns. That is, the argument is not designed to do good to any particular individual. It is designed rather "to prevent the harm that would be done to society by the weakness or vice of too many of its members."30

> It is obvious that an individual may by unrestricted indulgence in vice so weaken himself that he ceases to be a useful member of society. It is obvious also that if a sufficient number of individuals so weaken themselves, society will thereby be weakened.... If the proportion grows sufficiently large, society will succumb either to its own disease or to external pressures. A nation of debauchees would not in 1940 have responded satisfactorily to Winston Churchill's call to blood and toil and sweat and tears.31

Clor notes that Devlin's argument

> that citizen responsiblilities cannot be performed in the absence of certain virtues of self-discipline is most suitably addressed to polities in which the citizens participate in governing and in the making of public policy. A liberal government can be legitimately concerned with influences which undermine the moral requisites of its existence.32

Devlin's view does not require the State to get its directions from the highest possible ethical standards; it can take its bearings from minimal standards of decency. The third thesis seems to be the least objectionable one relating morality and society. Society at any level of generality cannot be inattentive to the maintainence of minimal standards of conduct without which the collapse of the society would be inevitable.

THE ENFORCEMENT OF MORALITY

Most people would agree that two extremes should be avoided with respect to the enforcement

114

of morals. The first extreme to shun is the total equating of morality and the law, a view that would subsume every immoral act under a criminal statute and allow a despot or equally fanatical majority to impose its morality upon the rest of society. Anyone seriously contemplating this kind of radical legal moralism must admit the possibility that once the State has obtained the power to enforce a total moral code, one's own religion or morality may be condemned as obscene and outlawed as a criminal practice.

The opposite extreme, in which the law is indifferent to immoral acts, is equally unacceptable. The writings of Murray Rothbard and David Friedman give us a glimpse into the moral inadequacies of a radically libertarian society. Rothbard does not believe, for example, that defamatory or libelous statements should be illegal.[33] Rothbard agrees that false statements about a person's conduct or character are immoral; but he does not believe they should be prohibited by law. Citizens in a Rothbardian society would be completely free to slander, libel, and defame anyone they please without any fear of legal sanctions. The lives, marriages, and careers of innocent people could be ruined by maliciously circulated untruths, without any hope of legal recourse.

David Friedman advocates the repudiation of laws covering the control of addictive drugs like heroin.[34] He believes that everyone who becomes a heroin addict does so "freely," a doubtful claim. Even if the person's subsequent addiction makes voluntary abstinence impossible, his original choice was free, Friedman thinks. Friedman writes, "Someone who becomes addicted by associating with other addicts has not been forcibly infected. He has seen a behavior pattern and chosen to adopt it.... The choice is up to him. His decision, like any act of free will, may be wrong. It is not involuntary."[35] The State should take no more action with regard to possible heroin addiction than it should in the case of potential converts to Christianity or political conservatism. If, Friedman concludes, "the addict is willing to trade his health or his life for a few years, or months, or minutes of drug-induced ecstasy, that is his affair. Part of freedom is the right of each of us to go to hell in his own fashion."36 Many will regard Friedman's contentions as the reductio ad absurdum of radical libertarianism. Unfortunately, he so oversimplifies and begs so many questions, libertarians ought to have the right to sue him for libeling their position. While people surely ought to have the freedom to go to hell if they choose, certain routes to damnation inevitably harm others in ways that should be a concern to any morally sensitive person. William F. Buckley, Jr. has argued that Friedman's heartless ideological purity holds

> that if the people of Harlem (or of wherever) choose to torture themselves to death, they have every 'right' to do so. If the alternatives are to spare Harlem and by extension the whole of New York City--and who knows the whole of the republic--or to spare the integrity of a Pure Theory, I would not hesitate. In fact I do not believe that the proper theory and practice exclude one another. The powers of the state are conceded in the matter of quarantine. It is rather an exertion of the imagination, than a travesty of the truth, to say that narcotics is a plague.... Does our enthusiasm for libertarian principle require of us such sociological blindness as prevents us from understanding that an individual who determines to destroy himself through drugs brings down a part of society with him--his sisters, brothers, parents, community....37

As vital as liberty is, there are some expressions of it that no decent society can permit. No civilized society treats morality as a totally private matter; all kinds of moral issues are the subject of criminal legislation. According to Irving Kristol,

116

the plain fact is that none of us is a complete civil libertarian. We all believe that there is some point at which the public authorities ought to step in to limit the 'self-expression' of an individual or a group, even where this might be seriously intended as a form of artistic expression, and even where the artistic transaction is between consenting adults. A playwright or theatrical director might, in this crazy world of ours, find someone willing to commit suicide on the stage, as called for by the script. We would not allow that--any more than we would permit scenes of real physical torture on the stage, even if the victim were a willing masochist. And I know of no one, no matter how free in spirit, who argues that we ought to permit gladiatorial contests in Yankee Stadium similar to those once performed in the Colosseum at Rome--even if only consenting adults were involved.[38]

Every civilized nation has recognized the need for some legal restraints on immoral conduct. They may not always have agreed precisely where the lines should be drawn. But they have agreed that the line ought to be drawn somewhere.

THE LIBERTY-LIMITING PRINCIPLES

Five different liberty-limiting principles are usually cited as the possible grounds on which human actions may be restrained by the law. (1) The principle of private harm, the most widely used principle, justifies State coercion in order to prevent direct, personal injury to other persons. (2) The principle of public harm allows State restraint in order to prevent harm to institutions and systems that serve the public interest. (3) The principle of offense would prohibit offensive conduct like loud noises, bad odors, public indecency, and invasions of privacy that may not be serious enough to be covered by the harm principle. (4) The principle of legal

117

paternalism allows the State to prevent actions in which people harm themselves. The difference between the private harm and paternalistic principles is the difference between preventing harm to others and preventing self-inflicted harm.
(5) The principle of legal moralism would give the State the right to prevent immoral acts not covered by one of the other principles.

I suppose that someone somewhere has advanced every possible combination of these five principles. But this would not begin to exhaust the possibilities since each of the principles is subject to a wide variety of interpretations.

The least objected-to principle is the private harm principle. To be sure, it was rejected by the Marquis de Sade, along with many others who have resided in penal or mental institutions. Any person who sees nothing wrong in actions that harm others may quite properly be regarded as a deviate. The principle most frequently opposed is legal moralism. My own view is that the principle of private harm is always applicable while the principles of public harm, paternalism, and offense are sometimes necessary. Since these four principles, properly interpreted, can cover any act for which a decent society requires legal sanctions, legal moralism can be eliminated as a liberty-limiting principle.

It is helpful to regard each of our four remaining principles as covering a continuum with the easy cases at each extreme and the hard cases in the middle. Using paternalism as an example,

LEGAL PATERNALISM

easy cases where paternalism does not justify restraint (e.g., mountain-climbing)	the hard cases	easy cases where paternalism does justify restraint (e.g., suicide)

118

Each principle applies, then, to a range of offenses with easy cases at both extremes. Suicide is an obvious case where the law should restrain self-harm while activities like mountain-climbing where the danger of self-harm is only probable are easily recognized exceptions to paternalism. The truly difficult cases where the arrival at a decision can be a formidable task can be approached from either extreme. For example, authorities seldom permit mountain-climbers to set out if they know bad weather is moving in. From the other end of the continuum, situations exist where a patient may be allowed to die through the refusal of certain "heroic measures." The existence of hard cases for all of our principles should not blind us to the fact that many decisions in these matters may be easy nor deceive us into thinking that no answers can be found to the hard cases.[39]

The need for a separate principle of offense to supplement the private harm principle is obvious, once one recognizes the right of people to protection from harmless offensive acts. The point requires some analysis of the relationship between harms and offenses. Joel Feinberg defines a harm as a violation of a human interest. He further defines an interest as "what is truly good for a person whether he desires it or not."[40] The kinds of interests with respect to which people can be harmed must be things in which they have a genuine stake. People have interests in their property, reputation, family relations, privacy, etc. Obviously, many things that interest us are trivial and unimportant. Someone who violated my interest in the score of a basketball game by falsely reporting the score can hardly be said to have harmed me in any serious way, unless his false report was designed to cheat me out of money I might have gambled on the game. The harms normally covered by the private harm principle are violations of interests in which people have a genuine stake. Offensive behavior, in contrast with harmful behavior, is a class of actions capable of inducing a variety of unpleasant,

119

uncomfortable, or disagreeable mental states such as disgust, shameful embarrassment or the irritation that accompanies bad smells or loud noises. If no distinction were drawn between harms and offenses, the applicability of the harm principle would be seriously affected. Offenses are so personal and the sensibilities of people so different that unless some difference between harms and offenses were recognized, there would be no practical limit on what might be forbidden on the basis of the harm principle. It seems clear that some human conduct can be patently offensive without actually harming anyone, that is, without violating some other person's genuine interest. Even John Stuart Mill acknowledged the importance of being free from offense when he wrote, "The liberty of the individual must be thus far limited; he must not make himself a nuisance to other people."41 While it may be debatable whether acts of defecation or copulation in public actually harm anyone and are thus covered by the private harm principle, they and other acts of public indecency would clearly be prohibited by the principle of offense.

As noted earlier with regard to paternalism, the offense principle also covers a continuum of activities ranging from those that are easy cases to those that are more difficult to decide. One factor that must be considered is the relative ease with which the offensive behavior can be avoided. It does not appear to be especially reasonable for a person to object to an offense if he can easily avoid the action. A person should not seek out ways to be offended.

> No one has a right to protection from the state against offensive experiences if he can effectively avoid those experiences with no unreasonable effort or inconvenience. If a nude person enters a public bus and takes a seat near the front, there may be no effective way for other patrons to avoid intensely shameful embarrassment...short of leaving the bus, which would be an unreasonable inconvenience. Similarly, obscene remarks over a

120

loudspeaker, homosexual billboards in Times
Square, and pornographic handbills thrust
into the hands of passing pedestrians all
fail to be reasonably avoidable.[42]

Other criteria that might apply to identifying
when offensive behavior should be restricted by
law would include a rather wide-spread agreement
by the community that the behavior is offensive
and the difficulty of restricting the behavior to
a limited area where it could be out of view of
the general public.

MORALS OFFENSES

Some of the most complex questions about
freedom arise in connection with the enforcement
of so-called "morals offenses." The most commonly
cited examples are sexual offenses like incest,
fornication, adultery, prostitution and sodomy,
along with nonsexual offenses like the mistreat-
ment of corpses, the desecration of a nation's
flag, and cruelty to animals.

Louis B. Schwartz has suggested that the difference between morals offenses and "ordinary
crimes" cannot be found in any special relation
morals offenses may have to morality. On the contrary he writes, "Virtually the entire penal code
expresses the community's ideas of morality, or at
least of the most egregious immoralities. To
steal, to kill, to swear falsely in legal proceed-
ings--these are certainly condemned as much by
moral and religious as by secular standards."[43]
Schwartz notes several other features about morals
offenses that does set them apart from more commonly recognized criminal offenses. For one thing,
morals offenses seem to lack an essential connection with social harm. The public security does
not appear to require the suppression of such
offenses. While the actions may occasionally harm
the agents, they have usually anticipated the possible harm and consented in advance to whatever
risk they faced. Even when the deeds offend

others, it is usually because the actions have been done in public, a factor that can be legislated by prohibitions against public indecency. Since the element of offensiveness is controllable by the principle of offense, the morals offenses that still raise problems for the law are those allegedly harmless immoralities practiced in private by consenting adults. Of course, this assumes that some immoral acts can be harmless, a point about which universal agreement is lacking. It is interesting to see the extent to which the enforcement of morality can be carried in such cases without resorting to legal moralism.

A helpful place to begin is with the 1957 publication in England of the Wolfenden Report. The Wolfenden Committee was a law reform commission charged to study and make recommendations about British laws making the practice of homosexuality a crime. Basing its conclusions primarily on the private harm principle, the committee concluded that existing laws against homosexual behavior should be relaxed. The committee argued for a distinction between private immorality and public indecency. Since sin and crime are not equivalent, the report maintained, there must be an area of morality that is not the business of the law. In actuality, however, the Wolfenden Report went beyond the private harm principle when it stated that the purpose of the law is

> to preserve public order and decency, to protect the citizen from what is offensive or injurious, and to provide sufficient safeguards against exploitation and corruption of others, particularly those who are specially vulnerable because they are young, weak in body or mind, inexperienced, or in a state of physical, official or economic dependence.44

This paragraph might well have been written by Anita Bryant. It affirms that no one has the right to flaunt his or her immorality in a way that is offensive or has the right to exploit and corrupt the morals of the immature, inexperienced, or dependent.

Shortly after its publication, the Wolfenden Report was criticized by Patrick Devlin, later Lord Devlin, whose views appeared in the book, The Enforcement of Morals.45 Three things about Devlin's argument are worth noting. (1) His objections were directed more to the reasoning of the committee, than to its conclusions. In other words, Devlin did not necessarily think that every homosexual act should be prosecuted. He objected primarily to the report's claim that the primary and perhaps exclusive function of the law is to protect people from harm. (2) Devlin himself did not actually defend the principle of legal moralism. (3) His own case rested on appeal to the principle of public harm. That is, he argued that the law was designed to do more than protect prospective victims from crime; it was also supposed to protect society. Society must of necessity affirm a public morality, and a violation of that public morality is a crime against society.46

Lord Devlin's major critic, Oxford philosopher H. L. A. Hart, called attention to problems in Devlin's appeal to a public morality.47 The details of Hart's attack are of less importance in this context than the fact that Hart himself found it necessary to appeal to something more than the private harm and the offense principles in order to cover the actions he believed should be illegal. Hart acknowledged a place for paternalism. He believed the law should be used to protect people from self-inflicted harms caused by such things as drug addiction.

I think the Wolfenden Report's appeal to the offense principle was sound. I also think Devlin was correct in recognizing the legitimate use of the law to protect the institutions of society. And I agree with Hart that paternalism is justified in certain cases. One difficulty with Hart was his failure to push the principle of

paternalism quite far enough. Bruce Kaye and
Gordon Wenham observe:

> If, then, the criminal law may legitimately
> adopt a somewhat 'paternalistic' role, as
> even Hart accepts, it would seem to follow
> that there should be no objection, in basic
> principle, to its being used to protect indi-
> viduals from any sort of injury, or to pre-
> serve the basic institutions of society (such
> as marraige and the family) from any attack
> on their integrity. But this does not mean
> that criminal sanctions ought in fact to be
> imposed in every such case; for there are a
> number of criteria which should always be
> taken into consideration before legislation
> is invoked.48

Hart approves of physical paternalism (restraining
self-inflicted harm to one's body) but opposes
moral paternalism. Why his inclination to tolerance in the case of moral harm? Are not people
harmed if their character is corrupted? Is not
moral corruption a form of injury or harm?

To summarize, the law should not punish
immoral actions simply because they are immoral.
But it does seem clear that some immoral acts war-
rant punishment on other grounds. A connection
between morality and the law does exist. But it
is not a hard and fast, or always visible line.
But use of the law to enforce morality is sometimes necessary.

How does one identify which forms of immorality should be prohibited by law? Several criteria
appear relevant. For one thing, legislators
should respect individual privacy as much as possible. They should also tolerate the maximum
amount of individual liberty consistent with maintaining the integrity of society. The law should
focus on minimal rather than on maximum standards
of conduct. And certainly, consideration should
be given to a law's enforceability. The enforcement of some laws might do more harm than the

offenses they regulate by producing, for example, massive invasions of privacy. Consideration should be given to the possibility that a contemplated law might be counter-productive and increase the likelihood of greater evils. Certainly this was the case with prohibition. It is one thing to identify the appropriate liberty-limiting principles and apply them to easy cases. It is quite another to apply them to the hard cases in ways that will result in fair and enforceable laws that will preserve the greatest possible liberty at the same time that they protect the essential interests of society. Legislators have erred both by acts of commission and omission. Mistakes will continue to be made. But both the individual and society have a stake in continuing efforts to mark out the point at which immoral actions should be prohibited by law.

CHAPTER FIVE

THREE ECONOMIC SYSTEMS

No discussion of freedom and justice would be complete without an examination of their application to economics. Questions about distributive justice could never arise apart from some economic system within which scarce goods can be acquired and exchanged. While social philosophers may debate about the most just way to divide people's holdings, the holdings themselves are the result of economic activity. Economic freedom is a necessary condition for personal and political liberty. No one can be free in the political sense if he lacks economic freedom. Economic freedom aids the existence and growth of political liberty by helping to check the concentration of too much power in the hands of too few people. As long as a large percentage of the people in a society exercise ownership control, power within that society will be more widely diffused. No one can be free when he is dependent upon others for the basic economic needs of life. If someone commands what a person can or cannot buy and sell, then a significant part of that individual's freedom has been abridged. Human beings who are dependent upon any one power for the basic essentials of life are not free. When that master becomes the State, obedience becomes a prerequisite to employment and to life itself.

The three basic economic systems that presently struggle for dominance are capitalism, socialism and the so-called mixed economy (or interventionism). Socialism and interventionism are statist systems while capitalism, properly understood, is not. The treatment of capitalism which begins this chapter has two primary objectives. First, I want to eliminate several widespread misconceptions of capitalism. Secondly, I want to provide a model of a free economy that can serve as the basis for contrast with the socialist and interventionist models. The chapter will then offer analyses and criticisms of the socialist and interventionist systems. The attack against capitalism will be the subject of chapter six.

CAPITALISM

The first obstacle that any attempt to provide a fair discussion of capitalism must overcome is the problem of terminology. For one thing, the very name most often given to the free market system ("capitalism") was actually coined by Marx as a term of reproach.

> As coined and circulated by Marxism, the term has retained up to the present so much of its hate-filled significance and class-struggle overtones that its usefulness for the purposes of scientific discussion has become extremely questionable. In addition, it provides us with only a very vague notion of the real essence of our economic system. Instead of promoting understanding, it merely arouses the emotions and obscures the truth.[1]

The availability of some other term or phrase, free of the negative emotive connotations of "capitalism," might well contribute to a more enlightened discussion of the issues. Unfortunately, no better term seems available, so that the most anyone can do apparently is make some effort to purify its usage.

The term "capitalism" presents other problems because it is used in two distinct ways. Sometimes the word is used in an abstract sense to refer to an ideal free market economy in which people exchange goods and services in an environment free from coercion, fraud, monopoly, and

128

statist interference with the exchange process.
It is important to note, as Von Mises writes, that
"The market is not a place, a thing, or a collective entity. The market is a process, actuated by
the interplay of the actions of the various individuals cooperating under the division of labor...
The forces determining the-continually-changing-
state of the market are the value judgments of
these individuals and their actions as directed by
these value judgments."[2]

"Capitalism" is also used to describe several
systems of exchange in the real world that approximate more or less the freedom of the ideal market. These systems differ, of course, in several
significant respects from the abstract perfection
of the ideal market. The relationship between the
ideal market and real economic exchanges is analogous to that between physiology and pathology.
No physician ever expects to find every organ in
every body functioning perfectly. His study of
physiology provides him with a standard by which
he can diagnose pathology. Likewise, the market
provides standards that can be used to judge the
health of economic practices in the real world.
Critics of capitalism frequently use the imperfections of existing systems to attack the model.
This is as silly as a doctor's discarding all his
physiology texts because he has never seen a perfectly healthy body.

Deviations from the market ideal occur for
several reasons. Frequently, they arise because
of statist interference with the market process.
Aberrations also occur because of defects in human
nature. Human beings naturally crave security and
guaranteed success, values not found readily in a
free market. Genuine competition always carries
with it the possibility of failure and loss. Consequently, the understandable human preference for
security leads men to avoid competition whenever
possible, encourages them to operate outside of
the market, and induces them to subvert the market
process through behavior that is often questionable and dishonest. Monopoly is one manifestation

of this human propensity to escape the uncertainty and insecurity of the market through the attainment of unfair advantage and special favor.

The Marxist claim that the market leads inevitably to monopoly is logically false. By definition, the market cannot co-exist with monopoly. It is impossible for the market to generate monopolies. Monopolies result from two other causes: (1) the human propensity to escape the uncertainty of the market; and (2) the existence of the only organization powerful enough to permit monopolies to exist, namely, the State. Historically, it is impossible to point to any single monopoly that did not arise as a result of special favors from government.[3] The way to terminate monopolies is for the State to end its practice of dispensing privileged treatment.

Assessments of capitalism differ widely, of course. Many of the more important objections to the system will be noted in chapter six. The remarks of John Hospers, professor of philosophy at the University of Southern California, are typical of those who support the market system.

Of all the institutions created in America, the one that has contributed most to the well-being of its inhabitants, more even than any of its institutions of government, is the free-enterprise system. Its beneficiaries are largely ignorant of it; many people, who are its beneficiaries, rail against it; yet it has provided more people with a high standard of living, by far, than any other system ever devised by man. The most ordinary things, which even the poorest people in America take for granted, were either non-existent or extreme luxuries in pre-industrial times. Because of free enterprise, and the technology which it developed, many times more people can live on the face of the earth than had ever been dreamed possible before.[4]

"Capital" is a word used to refer to any resource employed to produce other goods. Resources that can be used as capital include land, labor, and tools (which includes complex arrangements of tools such as factories). An additional resource not always recognized as capital is entrepreneurial competence, the ability to bring together other resources in ways that result in a product and make a profit. Capitalists believe that the limited resources that can be used to produce goods should be privately owned. They believe further that those who have the right of ownership in capital should have the right to transfer ownership. They also believe in freedom of enterprise, viz., that any individual or collection of individuals engaged in business should be free to obtain limited resources in a market and be free to sell the products that result from their use of the resources. They believe the State should not enter the market to set wages and prices. The process of the market is enough to insure sufficient competition. Entry to the market by new sellers is effectively restrained only when governmental action such as regulation or licensure gives earlier entrants a monopolistic advantage.[5]

A market economy begins by assuming a system of human rights such as the right to make decisions and the right to hold and exchange property. The things people freely exchange on the market are things to which they must have had prior rights. The market requires a limited State whose function is the protection of the rights that constitute the background of the market. People should be protected from fraud, misrepresentation, violence, theft, and other criminal acts.

One of the most important roles of the market is its function as an instrument for gathering and transmitting information. Each participant in the market process can receive signs or indicators of what needs other people want satisfied at a particular time and for a particular price. Without these indicators, the agent in the market would

131

never know which needs of other people he should aim to satisfy. The prices at which goods and services are selling is one such indicator which supplies important information telling each person in the market how best to direct his own efforts. The key to market exchange at any given moment is price. When people's wants are matched by a price they are willing and able to pay, they will buy. When a seller can make a profit (or avoid a greater loss) at this price, he will sell. Without the market mechanism, there would be no way to know the needs and wants of more than a few people. Statist attempts to circumvent the market process and control an entire economic system from some central agency have been notorious failures. The success of some in the market provides indicators that point to directions others should take if they desire similar success. That is, they should provide some service or product at a given price. Of course, when that part of the market becomes too crowded, the signals will change and the wise agent will be ready to switch his activity in accordance with the new signals. The market offers special rewards to those entrepreuneurs who are wise or lucky enough to tap new markets. The informational function of the market is negated by governmental intervention. Factors such as prices and interest rates which might tell the wary agent something in an unhampered market become, following the manipulations of the interventionist, distorted and misleading signals that can provide no clear direction. Governmental intervention that effectively nullified the signals from this mechanical process contributed to every economic crisis in America's history.[6]

The role of the State should be the same with respect to both economic and political freedom. The Rule of Law is a necessary condition for both kinds of liberty. The market requires a framework of laws which inform agents in the market which actions are legal. People require protection of their rights in the market, a protection that requires the existence of a minimal State that observes the Rule of Law. According to Hayek, support for the free market does "not mean that government should never concern itself with any economic matters."[7] Governmental actions that are inconsistent with the Rule of Law must, of course, be denounced and corrected. Governmental actions consistent with the Rule of Law must be evaluated in terms of their expediency. Those that are inexpedient, counter-productive, or harmful should be avoided. Capitalism is anti-statist because it rejects statist intervention that subjects the market process to tampering that negates the market's vital informational function and to tinkering that results in social costs that far outweigh the presumed advantages. Inflation which is always the result of the State's increasing the money supply is one social evil that results from such tinkering. As Henry Hazlitt observes, there is an obvious difference

> between a general undiscriminatory system of laws against force and fraud, on the one hand, and specific interventions in the market economy on the other. Some of these specific interventions may indeed "remedy" this or that specific "evil" in the short run, but they can do so only at the cost of producing more and worse evils in the long run.[8]

The statist interventions inherent in socialism and the mixed economy are interventions of the second type. It is to these kinds of intervention and the economic systems that embody them to which we turn next.

SOCIALISM

Like many of the other key terms encountered in this study, "socialism" is not an univocal word. It is a name given to a complex variety of ideologies united in their common opposition to something they call "capitalism." The correctness of socialist perceptions of capitalism varies widely, but rarely approximates reality. Whatever

133

capitalism is, socialists regard it as immoral, irrational, and exploitative. In their view, while capitalism stresses the pursuit of profit, it de-emphasizes basic human values by pandering to greed, materialism, and selfishness.

The various forms of socialism differ, in one sense, in the degree of centralized control they seek to impose on a nation's life and economy. In the case of the state socialisms of Russia, China, Cuba, East Germany, and Bulgaria, the centralized control could hardly be more total and more ruthless. Such state socialisms are a frequent source of embarassment to many professedly anarchistic socialists in the West who act as though there is room for non-statist forms of socialism at the opposite end of the spectrum. It seems unlikely that non-statist forms of socialism are feasible except in occasional and isolated communes that are sheltered by environs that provide the commune with state-funded protection and market-produced goods. Between the ominous and unavoidable presence of totalitarian socialist States on the one hand and the illusions of non-statist socialisms on the other, there exists a wide variety of economic systems that claim to be socialist but which are best viewed as types of economic interventionism.

Many contemporary apologists for socialism in the West are peddling politico-economic systems that have never yet existed on this planet.[9] Common sense ought to suggest that their utopian dreams never will be attained in the real world. As one sample of contemporary socialist rhetoric, consider Michael Lerner's prophecy: "Probably one of the first actions of a socialist government would be to make free such essential services as health care, transportation, utilities, and housing. All forms of cultural activity would be free."[10] Such claims must have great appeal for dullards. The author conveniently neglects to tell how hospitals, airplanes, automobiles, gasoline and bricks will suddenly become free in his socialist society. Under the mantle of the

socialist's marvelous system of double-talk,
everything paid for by forcibly extracted taxes
will simply be called free.

One thing that makes a competent evaluation
of socialism difficult is its chameleon-like quality. Whenever a particularly embarassing problem
is noted, socialists demur that that is not what
they mean by socialism. After the non-market
forms of socialism that prevailed sixty years ago
were shown to be untenable, socialists altered the
nature of their system to make it compatible with
some kind of market process, a change that is normally ignored in histories of the socialist movement. When contemporary cynics point accusingly
at the elitism and imperialism of Russian socialism, many Western socialists protest that their
system is different. In the words of one contemporary socialist, the state socialisms found in
Eastern Europe and the Soviet Union are to true
socialism what "the monsters of the paleolithic
era are to present animal species: clumsy, abor-
tive, prototypes."[11] As the socialist,
Michael Lerner advises, "We do not believe that
socialism now exists in any country in the
world."[12]

During the first two decades of the twentieth
century, the term "socialism" meant non-market
socialism, an economic system incompatible with
any process that would allow the factors of production to be determined by a market. Socialist
theorists in those years clearly regarded socialism and any market process as mutually exclusive.

These were the days when authoritative
socialist theoreticians dreamed of the
Naturalwirstschaft, a society without markets
or money, where the planners would run the
whole of the industry as though it were
Crusoe's island, using only technological
calculations "in kind."[13]

Socialists predicted that their non-market system
would far surpass the productivity of a market

135

system and, in the bargain, make superior living
standards possible for far more people.

About 1920, Ludwig Von Mises advanced the
argument that socialism is not only undesirable
but also impossible, because it makes economic
calculation impossible. According to Mises, production could never be attuned to human wants
without markets to set prices. The impossibility
of precise measures of cost-accounting under
socialism would result in general impoverishment.
Mises' argument involved three major steps.

First, Mises argued that economic calculation
is necessary for economic activity. Without economic calculation, there can be no economic activity such as buying and selling. Before people buy
and sell, they must calculate whether it is in
their interest to complete the contemplated trans-
actions. A person might desire both x and y, but
be unable to afford both. How could a rational
decision be made without some idea of the compara-
tive costs of the two items?

Secondly, pricing is necessary for economic
calculation. Decisions about whether to buy or
not require some indication of the costs. Without
an accurate barometer of how a person will end up
after the exchange, one could not make a rational
decision. The basic indicator that signals to
people when they should or should not engage in
economic activity is price.

Thirdly, Mises maintained that the market is
a necessary condition for pricing. In theory,
some central planning agency functioning in a
totally controlled economy without a market could
place a price on any item. The problem is not
just pricing items, but putting on the right
prices, that is, prices high enough to at least
cover costs and low enough to induce people to
buy. Market prices result from supply and demand.
In the market, a merchant can offer his wares at
any price he wants. His problem is whether or not
he will find any buyers at that price. If he does

not and still wishes to sell, he must lower his
price. Without markets, economic activity would
become chaotic and result in drastic inefficiencies and distortions. Von Mises' theoretical
attack found empirical support in the Bolshevik
attempt to establish non-market socialism in Russia between 1918 and 1921, when millions starved
as a result of the experiment.[14]

Non-market socialism is seldom touted anymore.
Out of embarassment, one supposes, history books
tend to ignore the early non-market forms of
socialism. Mises would seem to deserve some credit, even from the socialists, for compelling them
to reckon with the need for market pricing mechan-
isms. Contemporary socialists either ignore the
Misean attack or else they play a remarkable game
of scholarly legerdemain. In this latter case,
exaggerated claims are made on behalf of one or
two feeble attempts to answer the Misean argument.
Such an approach frequently appeals to the efforts
of a socialist economist named Oscar Lange to
introduce the equivalent of a market system into
socialism. What the so-called market socialisms
were supposed to have shown is how a central planning agency could vary prices by a process of
trial and error, the key being the rate at which
the factory's inventory would be depleted. Steele
comments:

> In fact, Lange's system is neither a mar-
> ket nor central planning. It is best classi-
> fied as a simulated market.... Everyone would
> pretend that there was a market and act as if
> there were a market, but there would be no
> market in actuality. Such a proposal might
> have immediately prompted the thought that if
> the pretense were to achieve the same results
> as the real thing, it might have to become
> the real thing. This notion of a pretend
> market was obscured by Lange's simultaneous
> advocacy of the marginal rule. It is only
> because no one really makes losses that
> Lange's managers can ignore the pursuit of
> profits. Discussion of the marginal rule

often went on without clearly establishing
whether its setting was the real market or a
pretend market.[15]

For example, the internal operations of a factory
cannot be organized without reference to external
markets. How does a factory decide whether it is
cheaper to manufacture half-finished goods within
the factory or perhaps buy them more cheaply from
some other factory? Without a system of markets,
there is no way to know. While socialism wants to
eliminate any basis for determining profit and
loss, such considerations cannot be abolished
without destroying the rational basis for all economic calculation. The failure of socialist
attempts to circumvent the problem by establishing
simulated markets is noted by Henry Hazlitt.

> A number of socialists think they can dupli-
> cate the functions and efficiencies of the
> free market by imitating the free market in a
> socialist system--that is, in a system in
> which the means of production are in the
> hands of the State. Such a view rests on
> mere confusion of thought. If I am a govern-
> ment commissar selling something I don't
> really own, and you are another commissar
> buying it with money that really isn't yours,
> then neither of us really cares what the
> price is. When, as in a socialist or commu-
> nist country, the heads of mines and facto-
> ries, of stores and collective farms, are
> mere salaried government bureaucrats who buy
> foodstuffs or raw materials from other
> bureaucrats and sell their finished products
> to still other bureaucrats, the so-called
> prices at which they buy and sell are mere
> bookkeeping fictions. Such bureaucrats are
> merely playing an artificial game called
> 'free market.' They cannot make a socialist
> system work like a free-enterprise system
> merely by imitating the so-called free-market
> feature while ignoring private property.[16]

Hazlitt points out that most socialist countries

including Russia practice this imitation of a free market pricing system. But, he adds, the only reason the socialist's imitation market economy works, the only reason socialist economies can function at all, is

> because its bureaucratic managers closely watch what commodities are selling for on free world markets, and artificially price their own in conformity. Whenever they find it difficult or impossible to do this, or neglect to do it, their plans begin to go more seriously wrong. Stalin himself once chided the managers of the Soviet economy because some of their artificially-fixed prices were out of line with those on the free world market.[17]

Von Mises did not deny that rational action might still be possible under socialism with regard to small and insignificant matters. But under a system that ignored the factors of profit and loss, it would be impossible for production to be consciously economical. Rational economic production would be impossible. "All economic change, therefore, would involve operations the value of which could never be predicted beforehand nor ascertained after they had taken place. Everything would be a leap in the dark. Socialism is the renunciation of rational economy."[18] Von Mises regarded his argument as unanswerable.

> It is therefore nothing short of a full acknowledgement of the correctness and irrefutability of the economists' analysis and devastating critique of the socialists' plans that the intellectual leaders of socialism are now busy designing schemes for a socialist system in which the market, market prices for the factors of production, and catallactic competition are to be preserved. The overwhelmingly rapid triumph of the demonstration that no economic calculation is possible under a socialist system is without precedent in the history of human thought.

139

The socialists cannot help admitting their
crushing final defeat. They no longer claim
that socialism is matchlessly superior to
capitalism because it brushes away markets,
market prices, and competition. On the contrary. They are now eager to justify socialism by pointing out that it is possible to
preserve these institutions even under
socialism. They are drafting outlines for a
socialism in which there are prices and com-
petition.19

Socialism, therefore, presents us with the picture
of a system of planning in which planning is
impossible. Without making major concessions to a
market process, or without imitating prices on the
free market, socialist economies would quickly
fall into chaos.

SOCIALISM AND HUMAN FREEDOM

The irrationality of an economic system that
makes economic activity impossible should be
grounds enough for rejection. Equally serious is
the frequently made allegation that socialism is
incompatible with human liberty. In this connection, the arguments of Friedrich Hayek's well-
known book, The Road to Serfdom, deserve careful
study.20 The totalitarian implications of socialist thought have been readily acknowledged by the
Marxist, Herbert Marcuse.

Marcuse was an unsparing critic of all
advanced industrial societies, especially the
United States. The details of his critique are
not important in this context. What is important
is the question, "Why don't the people who live in
these corrupt societies do something about it?"
Marcuse's answer was that they couldn't. Karl
Marx had believed that the workers would carry the
revolution. But in Marcuse's view, Marx failed to
see how the workers would become part of the
Establishment. Marcuse believed that the worker
in an advanced industrial society becomes

140

corrupted by the affluence of the society until he has the same values as the bourgeoisie.

According to Marcuse, modern technology in societies like America eliminates dissent and conflict that might arise in less advanced societies, by raising false needs and providing false satisfactions. It enslaves people by deceiving them into thinking that the things it gives them are what they really want--better homes and appliances, faster cars, more leisure and luxury. In effect, Americans are so completely dominated, controlled, preconditioned, indoctrinated, and brainwashed that they cannot even recognize their bondage. As Marcuse put it, "The so-called consumer economy and the politics of corporate capitalism have created a second nature of man which ties him libidinally and aggressively to the commodity form." Man becomes so obsessed by the gadgets he wants to possess, handle, consume, and renew that he ignores the possibility that this obsession may destroy him. The possibility of man in an advanced industrial society rising up against the hand that feeds him is faint, perhaps nonexistent, because "the second nature of man thus militates against any change that would disrupt and perhaps even abolish this dependence of man on a market ever more densely filled with merchandise."[21]

Marcuse attacked this false mass contentment by claiming that the goods produced by the capitalist system provide false satisfaction. First, the system manipulates people into wanting things and then it seduces them into buying them. And then, through such devices as advertising, it increases these wants until the desire to consume becomes compulsive, irrational, and inhuman. The belief of the average man that he is happy only shows how total his bondage is. The things that make man believe he is happy (the electric can openers, the indoor toilets, the diet colas, the boysenberry-flavored breakfast cereals) are the very chains that bind him. Marcuse knew that the members of a capitalist society were not really happy. It made no difference that the individual

141

identified with his needs and believed they were
his. Marcuse knew that the needs were the false
product of a repressive society.

What was needed, Marcuse claimed, was for men
to free themselves from false needs and false consciousness to true needs and a true consciousness.
What was required was a new type of man who could
not be seduced by affluence. "Men must come to...
find their way from false to true consciousness,
from their immediate to their real interest. They
can do so only if they live in need of changing
their way of life, of denying the positive, of
refusing. It is precisely this need which the
established society manages to repress to the
degree to which it is capable of 'delivering the
goods' on an increasingly large scale, and using
the scientific conquest of nature for the scientific conquest of man."[22] Later in the same book,
Marcuse continued, "If and when men and women act
and think free from [their identification with
their false fathers]...they will have broken the
chain which linked the fathers and the sons from
generation to generation." The causes that have
turned human history into a history of domination
and servitude are economic and political. But
since these causes "have shaped the very instincts
and needs of men, no economic and political
changes will bring this historical continuum to a
stop unless they are carried through by men who
are physiologically and psychologically able to
experience things, and each other, outside the
context of violence and exploitation."[23]

It is not enough, however, for Marcuse to
argue that men must free themselves from the
oppressive influence of false needs imposed by a
repressive society; he ought also to have
explained how this could be done. And more impor-
tantly, he should have shown, given his analysis
of man's lost estate in the advanced industrial
society, that the attainment of liberation and
autonomy is possible. Marcuse may have backed
himself into a corner with no way out.

In the last analysis, the question of what are true and false needs must be answered by the individuals themselves, but only in the last analysis; that is, if and when they are free to give their own answer. As long as they are kept incapable of being autonomous, as long as they are indoctrinated and manipulated (down to their very instincts), their answer to this question cannot be taken as their own. By the same token, however, no tribunal can justly arrogate to itself the right to decide which needs should be developed and satisfied. Any such tribunal is reprehensible, although our revulsion does not do away with the question: how can the people who have been the objective of effective and productive domination by themselves create the conditions of freedom?[24]

Indeed! This was just the question that Marcuse needed to and yet failed to answer. Marcuse's problem stemmed from his claim that there was no way for the system to correct itself because it was impossible for those dominated by the system to free themselves from it.

The plot is thickened by two additional ingredients that seem to make liberation impossible. First, Marcuse argued that social change could not take place through democratic means because democracy contributes to the plight of society by lulling people into decisions that are against their best interests. Advanced industrial societies like the United States appear tolerant of minority views because they know that those views cannot have any effect. Men are not free when they vote and make political decisions. because, according to Marcuse, all who start out under the domination of a repressive society are preconditioned receptacles; they are incapable of criticizing the society or even of heeding a legitimate criticism.

This led Marcuse to his doctrine of "Repressive Tolerance."[25] Because American society is in

such perilous danger, Marcuse came to believe that
the suspension of free speech and free assembly
was justified. After all, there is no real value
to freedom of speech; it only insures the propaga-
tion of lies. Truth is carried by revolutionary
minorities like Marcuse's disciples. Therefore,
tolerance should be withdrawn from all those who
disagree with Marcuse and extended only to those
who make what he called the Great Refusal. Social
change can be brought about not by democratic
legality but by extra-democratic rebellion. Marcuse wanted to replace democratically supported
elites with an elite of his own choosing. In his
words, "Liberating tolerance, then, would mean
intolerance against movements from the Right, and
toleration of movements from the Left. As to the
scope of this tolerance and intolerance...it would
extend to the stage of action as well as of discussion and propaganda, of deed as well as of
word."26 Oddly enough, Marcuse admitted that even
if his totalitarian measures were put into practice and his followers succeeded in destroying
existing society, he could not be sure what would
follow.27 The questions raised by Marcuse's theory
are obvious: How does Marcuse's elite free itself
from the conditioning that blinds everyone else?
And who will provide deliverance from the repres-
siveness of Marcuse's elite? Such considerations
have led several interpreters of Marcuse to see
signs of a neo-Nazi mentality in his position.28

While the first difficulty Marcuse saw in
achieving liberation was the failure of the democratic process, the second problem was the power-
lessness of critical social theory to criticize.
"Confronted with the total character of the
achievements of advanced industrial society, critical theory is left without the rationale for
transcending this society."29 The very categories
of critical theory were developed within the
structure of the system. Furthermore, those who
might give the criticism are preconditioned by the
system. And finally, those who might otherwise be
influenced by a criticism of their society are so
brainwashed that they cannot appreciate the force

144

of or understand the nature of the criticism.
Thus, there is no one to give the critique, no one
to understand, and no critical theory in terms of
which the needed critique can be given. Things
indeed look hopeless. But for whom? Perhaps Marcuse created a greater problem for himself than he
did for capitalism.[30]

Just when things looked hopeless, Marcuse
began to see signs of the Great Refusal all over
the place: the revolutions in Vietnam, Cuba, and
China; guerrilla activities in Latin America;
strains in the fortress of corporate capitalism;
stirrings among ghetto populations; and last, but
not least, student uprisings. But there was also
a huge and embarrassing lacuna in Marcuse's argument. How, given the total domination of the
repressive society, was this opposition possible?
Since Marcuse was claiming that all people living
in advanced industrial societies are controlled,
manipulated, and brainwashed to the extent that
they think they are happy, are unable to see their
society's faults, and are unable to appreciate
criticisms of their society, then Marcuse's thesis
is self-defeating in the sense that no one,
including himself, could have obtained knowledge
of the thesis. And even granting that Marcuse's
books could be the result of a miracle, no one
else, according to his theory, could have understood him.

This brief detour into Marcusian socialism is
enlightening for several reasons. While almost
all socialists profess that their system will
expand human liberty, Marcuse acknowledged the
deceit of such claims. Even the socialist who
dreams of a socialistic democracy at the end of
the transformation of society, must assent to the
use of repressive measures against any who would
impede his noble goals. Moreover, Marcuse's system exhibits the same self-defeating trait as
socialist economics. Surely, it would appear,
whatever attraction socialism has for its many
disciples, its allure can not be based on rational
grounds.

INTERVENTIONISM

The economic system so frequently criticized in the United States does not happen to be capitalism. This fact is conveniently ignored every time some weakness of the system results in blame being placed on the free market system. Interventionism is the belief that statist intervention in economic matters can successfully achieve desired results while falling short of the total controls necessary under socialism. A mixed economy is supposed to be a workable third alternative to the freedom of the market and the total state control of socialism. The State, interventionists claim, only interferes with the market process when necessary to attain some desirable social goal or to avoid some social evil. The interventionist is convinced that many humanitarian goals are unattainable without resorting to occasional and partial statist controls.

The fundamental defect of the mixed economy was uncovered by Ludwig Von Mises. According to Mises, no logically third alternative to a free market and socialism is possible; no compromise between a market economy and socialism is practical. Partial governmental controls must inevitably fail, which will result in an already bad situation becoming worse. According to Mises,

> The effect of intervention is the very opposite of what it was meant to achieve. If government is to avoid the undesirable consequences it cannot stop with just market interference. Step by step it must continue until it finally seizes control over production from entrepreneurs and capitalists.... Government cannot be satisfied with a single intervention, but is driven on to nationalize the means of production. This ultimate effect refutes the notion that there is a middle form of organization, the "regulated" economy, between the private property order and the public property order.[31]

Interference with market processes will not only fail to attain the interventionist's goals, it will produce conditions worse than those he sought to alter through his controls. This is not to say that things may not appear better in the short run. But in the long run, the unforeseen consequences will be worse. Several examples will make this clearer.

Imagine a State that decides that the price of eggs is too high. Because the State wants to make it easier for poor people to buy eggs, the bureaucrats decide that the imposition of controls on the price of eggs will benefit the poor. Such statists find it easy to congratulate themselves for their humanitarianism and condemn the greedy entrepreuneurs who are too interested in making a profit to care that a basic human need is going unmet. Because the government cares, it will now act to alleviate the need.

Suppose that the market price for eggs is a dollar a dozen and that the State decides that the quickest way to make eggs more easily available to the poor is to pass a law making it illegal to retail eggs for more than 75¢ a dozen. As soon as the ceiling price drops below the market price, all kinds of unforeseen consequences will occur. First of all, marginal egg producers will find that they are losing money. In every case where a producer's costs (for chicken feed, electricity, gasoline, etc.) exceed his profit under the newly imposed price-ceiling, the State's interference will result in many of them leaving the market. Rather than continue to lose money, many marginal producers will probably sell their chickens to Colonel Sanders and find something more profitable to do. Perhaps they will even give up farming when they discover they can do just as well on welfare.

After the State imposed price-ceiling forces many marginal farmers out of the egg business, fewer eggs will be available, a result that is precisely the opposite of what the bureaucrats

originally intended. The statists believed that
their intervention into the market would make eggs
more available. But as things have turned out,
their action has only made eggs more scarce. At
this point, the State has two choices. It might
decide to regulate prices all the way down the
line. That is, the State might decide that it can
retain the price-ceiling on eggs and still keep
marginal producers in the market by imposing additional controls on the major costs of the chicken
farmer. If the marginal chicken farmer cannot
stay in business because of the high cost of
grain, the way to solve the problem is to impose
new price controls on chicken feed. But this simply pushes the problem back to the level of the
grain farmer. If he cannot make a profit growing
grain, he will turn to something else, which will
have the effect of making grain more scarce. It
soon becomes obvious that the only way governmental intervention into the market can succeed is if
it becomes total control. But this, of course,
would be socialism and mark an end of any experiment in a mixed economy. What began as an innocent, humane, benevolent (and foolish) governmental attempt to make eggs available to more people
has not only failed, but has introduced total
state control over an entire industry.

The other choice for the statist (other than
continuing with partial controls that repeatedly
fail) is to admit that he made a mistake and end
the controls. Naturally, the removal of controls
will produce a number of problems until the disastrous effects of the intervention are gradually
overcome through the ordinary processes of the
market. In the case of controls on the price of
eggs, a removal of the ceiling price in conjunc-
tion with the State-induced shortage will result
in a dramatic but temporary rise in the price of
eggs. The higher price, for which the State is
responsible, will cause hardship among the poor
people it was trying to help. But the higher
price will also be a signal to new producers that
this is now a propitious time to enter the egg
business. Eventually, the increased supply will

begin to meet the demand and the market price will drop. But all this will take time and during the interval, many more people will be forced to go without eggs than before the State's interference with the market process.

Mises' argument against interventionism, then, maintains that any statist intervention with the market must proceed in either of two directions. Either the State must return to a free market economy and allow the damages resulting from its intervention to ease gradually; or else the State can keep adding more and more controls until all economic freedom ends. There can be no consistent, successful middle ground between the market and socialism.

But interventionists are a remarkably resourceful group. Whenever confronted by the failures of their partial controls, they have a predictable response. The failures of the mixed economy are offered as evidence that previous controls did not go far enough; what is really required is more interference with the market, not less. In other words, it is always the market process and never interventionism that receives the blame for failure. Through this remarkable slight of hand, past failures are never regarded as reasons for abandoning interventionism. Rather, the mistakes of the past are used as justifications for even more total controls in the future. And so, interventionism moves increasingly closer to the total controls of socialism.

The history of America's cotton production since 1955 provides another example of Von Mises' thesis. The United States produced half of the world's cotton (some 18 million bales) in 1955. But in 1969, only 11 million bales were harvested. This dramatic decline resulted from growing competition from foreign cotton growers and synthetic fabrics. But what gave added strength to their intrusion into the market? According to a 1969 article in Time magazine,

Ironically, both synthetic makers and foreign
growers were given access to cotton's domain
as an unforeseen result of U.S. Government
policy. The troubles began with rigid,
Depression-born price supports, which eventually reached a peak of 32¢ a pound in 1955.
They were aimed at propping the growers'
income, but in the process they raised the
price of U.S. cotton above the going world
rate. The government's solution to that problem was to subsidize exports, beginning in
1956. That move, in turn, created a crisis
for domestic millers, who complained that
they had to pay more for U.S. cotton than
competing foreign mills. Washington's answer
was to add a third subsidy, this time for the
millers.[32]

Time proceeded to note eventual changes in this
cumbersome three-tiered support program, but the
damage was already done. Foreign growers had
already become established. As Time concluded,
the cotton industry "has been harmed more than
helped by the complicated schemes spun by federal
bureaucrats...."

Minimum wage laws are a further example of
how interventionist policies are counter-
productive. Defenders of minimum wage legislation
claim that the State must intervene in the market
to insure that employees, especially disadvantaged
and unskilled workers, get a 'fair' wage. What
this interference does, however, is only increase
unemployment among those workers whose productivity is too low to justify the minimum rate.[33]
Once again, statist intervention punishes the very
people it was supposed to help.

Perhaps the most damning consequence of modern interventionism is the growing affliction of
Western economies by simultaneous inflation and
recession. Murray Rothbard provides the background for this crisis.

For forty years we have been told, in the

textbooks, the economic journals, and the
pronouncements of our government's economic
advisors, that the government has the tools
with which it can easily abolish inflation or
recession. We have been told that by jug-
gling fiscal and monetary policy, the government can "fine-tune" the economy to abolish
the business cycle and insure permanent prosperity without inflation.[34]

According to orthodox economic theory, any slowing
of the economy can be countered by the State's
"stepping on the gas" by increasing the money supply and/or federal spending. When inflation
becomes the problem, all the government has to do
is apply the brakes. But, Rothbard asks, "what
can the government do, what does conventional economic theory tell us, if the economy is suffering
a severe inflation and depression at the same
time? How can our self-appointed driver, Big Government, step on the gas and on the brake at one
and the same time?" Rothbard contends that "Conventional economic theory is bankrupt." Interventionist policies have created the current crisis
and are impotent to solve it. Any continuation of
the interventionism will only add to the woes.
Interventionist economists and politicians usually
profess great puzzlement as to the causes of
inflation. This is understandable since their
manipulations of the economy are its major cause.
Henry Hazlitt identifies the nature and cause of
inflation:

Inflation is an increase in the quantity
of money and credit. Its chief consequence
is soaring prices. Therefore inflation...is
caused solely by printing more money. For
this the government's monetary policies are
entirely responsible.... The causes of inflation are not, as so often said, "multiple and
complex," but simply the result of printing
too much money.... If, without an increase in
the stock of money, wage or other costs are
forced up, and producers try to pass these
costs along by raising their selling prices,

151

most of them will merely sell fewer goods.
The result will be reduced output and loss of
jobs. Higher costs can only be passed along
in higher selling prices when consumers have
more money to pay the higher prices.[35]

Additional attempts by the State to control the
inflation, short of stopping the government printing presses and the expansion of credit, cannot
stop the inflation.

> Price controls cannot stop or slow down
> inflation. They always do more harm. Price
> controls simply squeeze or wipe out profit
> margins, disrupt production, and lead to bot-
> tlenecks and shortages. All government price
> and wage control, or even "monitoring" is
> merely an attempt by the politicians to shift
> the blame for inflation on to producers and
> sellers instead of their own monetary poli-
> cies.[36]

Rothbard agrees with Hazlitt in holding "that per-
sistent inflation is brought about by continuing
and chronic increases in the supply of money,
engineered by the federal government."[37] This has
been possible since the beginning of the Federal
Reserve System in 1913 placed the supply of money
and bank credit entirely in the hands of the federal government. Inflation will never stop until
the governemnt ends its practice of debasing the
currency through legalized counterfeiting.

> Statist arguments that governmental interven-
> tion with the economy is absolutely necessary to
> maintain social stability and to enhance freedom
> and justice are at best a cruel joke. Any effort
> to produce a system of property hampered by gov-
> ernment controls will inevitably produce a crisis
> which must lead to a surrender to the total con-
> trols of socialism.

CONCLUSION

This chapter began by identifying some of the
basic features of a market economy. It argued
that the socialist alternative to a market economy
is self-defeating because socialism makes economic
calculation impossible. The only reason socialist
economies have not failed more frequently is
because of their access to pricing information
from markets in non-socialist countries. Attempts
to establish a mixed economy must also fail.
While partial controls will always result in the
interventionist's goals being frustrated, the
imposition of total controls would transform the
mixed economy into socialism. Neither socialism
nor interventionism appear justifiable on rational
grounds. But perhaps there are objections to a
market system so dramatic that alternatives to the
market must be pursued in spite of their apparent
irrationality. The next chapter will examine the
most important attacks against capitalism.

CHAPTER SIX

REASON, MORALITY AND THE MARKET

A consideration of the major arguments
against capitalism is relevant to the themes of
this book. For one thing, many of the criticisms
of a market economy conclude that capitalism must
be abolished or restricted because it is unjust or
because it restricts important human freedoms.
But defenders of the market counter that capitalism is an important bulwark of human liberty and
that the abolishment or curtailment of the economic freedom of the market will have serious
consequences for political freedom. Defenders of
the market also argue that the alleged injustices
of capitalism presuppose a narrow and arbitrary
sense of justice (i.e., distributive justice).
In effect, the critic of capitalism stacks the
deck: first, he defines "justice" so that it is
necessarily incompatible with the kinds of procedural justice provided by the market; and then he
claims to discover empirically a "truth" (i.e.,
that capitalism is unjust) that actually follows
tautologically from his premise. As Irving
Kristol explains,

> It is fashionable these days for social
> commentators to ask, "Is capitalism compati-
> ble with social justice?" I submit that the
> only appropriate answer is "No." Indeed,
> this is the only possible answer. The term
> "social justice" was invented in order not to
> be compatible with capitalism.
> What is the difference between "social
> justice" and plain, unqualified "justice?"
> Why can't we ask, "Is capitalism compatible
> with justice?" We can, and were we to do so,

we would then have to explore the idea of
justice that is peculiar to the capitalist
system, because capitalism certainly does
have an idea of justice.

"Social justice," however, was invented
and propagated by people who were not much
interested in understanding capitalism.
These were nineteenth century critics of cap-
italism--liberals, radicals, socialists--who
invented the term in order to insinuate into
the argument a quite different conception of
the good society from the one proposed by
liberal capitalism. As it is used today, the
term [social justice] has an irredeemably
egalitarian and authoritarian thrust. Since
capitalism as a socioeconomic or political
system is neither egalitarian nor authoritarian, it is in truth incompatible with "social
justice."1

As the chapter on justice made clear, it is highly
debatable whether attempts to apply the notion of
distributive justice to massive, complex, spontaneous situations like an entire society make
sense.

Claims that statist intervention with the
market will expand human freedom seem to depend on
the assumption that some kind of positive freedom
can be distinguished and defended. This assumption has already been shown to contain serious
difficulties. But perhaps the attack against the
market in the name of freedom can assume a different form. We have already noted Marcuse's
argument that because modern technology provides
ways for the capitalist elite to control and manipulate the desires of the masses, the freedom of
capitalism is an illusion. Under capitalism, the
masses are actually slaves. The last chapter
pointed out the serious problems that the proponent of this argument faces in making this claim
defensible.

Statists conveniently ignore a more significant way in which the notion of freedom relates to

economic issues. A typical American worker pays out approximately 40% of his income for visible and hidden taxes. This means that this typical individual is forced to work two days out of every five just to pay his taxes. If the State simply coerced people to work for it two days a week, for nothing, the difference between this enforced servitude and slavery would be difficult to discern.

Can the market be defended against the many attacks levelled against it? What follows is an attempt to identify and evaluate actual arguments against the market. What frequently pass as criticisms of the market are not arguments but sermons and slogans unsupported by anything remotely resembling reasons or evidence.

Israel Kirzner comments, "One of the most intriguing paradoxes surrounding modern capitalism is the hate, the fear, and the contempt with which it is commonly regarded. Every ill in contemporary society is invariably blamed on business, on the pursuit of private profit, on the institution of private ownership."[2] Capitalism is blamed for every evil in contemporary society including its greed, materialism and selfishness, the prevalence of fraudulent behavior, the debasement of society's tastes, the pollution of the environment, the alienation and despair within society, and the vast disparities in wealth. Even racism and sexism are treated as effects of capitalism. With such an easily identifiable cause of society's ills, it is little wonder the critic has such an easy solution, the replacement of capitalism by a "just economic system," a euphemism for some type of centrally controlled economy. Many such objections to the market result from a simple but clearly fallacious two-step operation. First, some undesirable feature is noted in a society in which a market economy functions. Then, it is simply asserted that capitalism is the cause of this feature. Logic texts call this the Fallacy of False Cause. Mere coincidence does not prove causal connection. Such critics of capitalism conveniently overlook the fact that many of the

157

undesirable features of capitalist societies also exist under socialism.

The cause of the anti-capitalist is helped to no small extent by his audience's inattention to two factors without which an understanding of many social problems is often impossible. The first of these is the history of the problem, i.e., the particular problem occurs at the end of a long chain of causes and effects. When social critics ignore the history of a problem, it is easy to overlook the degree to which past actions of the State have contributed to the problem. The second factor that is easily disregarded is the extent to which an economic system is precisely that, a system. In any genuine system, isolated actions that do not produce effects elsewhere in the order are rare. It is not difficult to observe numerous cases in a capitalist economy that are disturbing and deserving of criticism. No great effort is required to denounce immoral and unfair treatment of human beings. But it frequently requires long hours of study and reflection to reveal how the contemptible effect may have resulted from apparently innocent and well-intended pressures applied elsewhere in the system. It is natural for people's moral outrage in such cases to be expressed in the form of demands for immediate State action to remedy the situation. But the critic of capitalism should be honest to acknowledge those times when the injurious situation is the complex result of earlier statist intervention.

Fifteen arguments against capitalism will be noted. These will be divided into two major categories, viz., those that find capitalism immoral and those which judge it irrational. While I am quite sure that a number of possible arguments have been overlooked, I believe the lines of reasoning I take and the replies I suggest to cited arguments will be sufficient to handle the objections that may have been missed. Any omitted arguments will end up repeating errors similar to the arguments that are discussed.

THE ALLEGED IMMORALITY OF CAPITALISM

1. Capitalism is immoral because it contributed to the widespread misery of the working class in nineteenth century industrialized nations. Friedrich Hayek describes this objection as the

> one supreme myth which more than any other has served to discredit the economic system [of capitalism].... It is the legend of the deterioration of the position of the working classes in consequence of the rise of 'capitalism' (or of the 'manufacturing' or the 'industrial system').... The widespread emotional aversion to 'capitalism' is closely connected with this belief that the undeniable growth of wealth which the competitive order has produced was purchased at the price of depressing the standard of life of the weakest elements of society.[3]

Bertrand Russell typified those persuaded that early capitalism grew by feeding upon the misery of the working classes that it exploited. In Russell's words,

> The industrial revolution caused unspeakable misery both in England and in America. I do not think any student of economic history can doubt that the average happiness in England in the early nineteenth century was lower than it had been a hundred years earlier; and this was due almost entirely to scientific technique.[4]

Russell failed to inform his reader what evidence he had for his belief that the life of the poor in the eighteenth century was such a happy lark compared to the utter misery produced by the Industrial Revolution.

In 1954, Friedrich Hayek edited a book, Capitalism and the Historians, in which he challenged the accuracy of this collection of charges. He

159

pointed to a tremendous bias on the part of historians that has led many of them to ignore the
evidence that contradicts the simplistic thesis
that the misery of the nineteenth century poor can
be laid squarely at the doorstep of capitalism.
The undeniable misery of that century should be
seen as a continuation of the wretchedness of previous centuries superimposed on the particular
conditions of life in a society becoming increasingly industrialized. Instead of the poor starving in dirty hovels in the country, they were
starving in dirty city slums.

> Several generations of eighteenth- and
> nineteenth-century writers, clergymen, and
> assorted social critics tended to lay the
> blame for every social woe, real or imagined,
> at the factory doorstep. Many of the intel-
> lectuals during the Industrial Revolution
> looked about and suddenly noticed that there
> was poverty. But the poverty had been there
> all along. Why, then, the passionate dis-
> taste for the very system which was gradually
> improving man's material lot? Possibly capi-
> talism was its own worst enemy in this
> respect, for in raising the general standard
> of living it made more conspicuous the pov-
> erty that still remained.[5]

Poverty did not begin with the advent of capitalism. It may have become more obvious as more and
more of the middle class rose to modest affluence,
making the contrast between them and the poor more
apparent. Perhaps the poor were also more notice-
able because they flocked to urban areas where
work was to be found.

The use of child labor in the early years of
the Industrial Revolution is a legitimate target
of concern. But, once again, it is proper to ask
to what extent more general ills in society contributed to the problem. Everyone would prefer a
society in which children are free to play games
and pick flowers. Unfortunately, that choice was
not readily available in those years.

For many of these children the factory system
meant quite literally the only chance for
survival. Today, we overlook the fact that
death from starvation and exposure was a common fate prior to the Industrial Revolution,
for the pre-capitalist economy was barely
able to support the population. Yes, children were working. Formerly they would have
starved. It was only as goods were produced
in greater abundance at lower cost that men
could support their families without sending
their children to work.[6]

Was capitalism to blame for the miserable
housing conditions of nineteenth century England?
The enemy of the market seldom points out the
vital role the British State played in this matter.
For example, usury laws restricted housing by making it extremely difficult for builders to borrow
the money needed to build new housing. There was
also a heavy tax on bricks needed for housing as
well as a heavy duty on imported timber that might
have been used for such building. There was even
a tax on windows that penalized the owners of
buildings who sought to make more light and fresh
air available. Taxes on bricks and tiles also
restrained the construction of drains and sewers.

Were conditions really worse than in earlier
centuries? The evidence is certainly inconclusive
and hardly warrants the dogmatism of Lord Russell.
Was capitalism solely responsible for the wretched
lot of the nineteenth century poor? More attention should be given to the complicity of the
British State in this matter. The truth is, as
Hazlitt notes, that

Capitalism has enormously raised the level of
the masses. It has wiped out whole areas of
poverty. It has greatly reduced infant mor-
tality, and made it possible to cure disease
and prolong life. It has reduced human suffering. Because of capitalism, millions live
today who would otherwise have not even been
born. If these facts have no ethical

161

relevance, then it is impossible to say in
what ethical relevance consist.[7]

This first objection to capitalism can only be
advanced by those who carefully sift the evidence
to fit their pre-conceived prejudices.

2. <u>Capitalism is immoral because it exploits,
cheats and robs its own workers</u>. Probably every
adult American has heard this charge some time or
other. Possibly many unhappy employees have
believed that the claim was true, at least in the
case of their employer. No doubt, some of them
believed correctly. No one in his right mind
would suggest that examples of money-grubbing capitalists cheating their workers cannot be found.
But that does not happen to be the question. The
problem is whether such exploitation is endemic to
the system, whether there is something inherent in
the free market system that makes such exploitation necessary and unavoidable. Also relevant is
the issue of whether it is possible for the free
market to adopt measures that would allow workers
to have a greater share of the profits. As we
shall see, such policies are available, but are
frequently disdained by the workers themselves.

The charge that capitalism entails the
exploitation of the worker has been advanced in
two different forms. In the first of these, it
appears in classic Marxist thought in the guise of
the famous labor theory of value. Many Marxists
have believed that the profit of the capitalist
results from his paying his workers less than the
true value of what their labor produced. The theory has never commanded much respect because of
its gross oversimplification of the worker's true
situation. The theory, for example, ignores the
extent to which machines multiply the value of
that which human beings produce. A solitary
worker using only his own raw materials and his
own tools might have some justification for
believing that he deserved the full value of the
labor he expended on the product. But even this
claim would overlook the contribution made to a

162

product's value by the exchange process. The laborer could not be paid for his product until it is sold or exchanged. If the worker is forced to take time off from his manufacturing activity (we might suppose he is making tables) while he seeks a buyer for the table he has already made, the time he loses will be a cost. That is, if he can make one table a day, or five a week, for which he receives say $20 apiece, but must spend two days a week selling his tables, that exchange process has cost him two tables or forty dollars. Some people are better at different tasks than others. If the worker can entrust the selling of his tables to someone who is a better salesman (who can, let us say, sell the five tables in half a day), a division of labor is obviously to the worker's advantage. But it also seems clear that the value of the table (that for which it is exchanged) does not result exclusively from the labor that produced it. The exchange process affects the table's value as well. Therefore, even in the most primitive of situations, the labor theory of value is oversimplified because it ignores other factors that affect the value of commodities.

But what about a more complex and realistic situation where a worker, using raw materials purchased and transported to him at someone else's expense and using machines paid for at some risk by an enterprising entrepreneur, is enabled to make ten tables a day? Does his increased productivity entitle him to ten times more pay? Marx's labor theory of value ignores the extent to which machines multiply a worker's productivity. Certainly, someone had to pay for the machines; someone had to invent them. Someone had to have the initiative to take the risks involved in investing money for the whole enterprise. It takes a warped moral intuition to contend that the person who made these investments and took these risks deserves no return from the added productivity of the workers who use his capital. It seems clear that if capitalism is to be condemned for robbing its workers, it must be on some basis other than the labor theory of value.

But the claim of worker-exploitation might be made in a different way. Perhaps it can be argued that capitalists exploit their workers by claiming excess profits. That is, even if it is conceded that the capitalist is entitled to some return on his risk and investment, there is a line between a fair return and obscene profits. In most cases (except those in which the intervention of a State has given some corporation a marked advantage over its competition), excessively large profits would be a temporary circumstance. If some company through insight or luck were fortunate to gain such dominance of a market as to produce huge profits, this fact would quickly lead other entrepreneurs to enter the same market. The history of American business is full of companies that gained an uncommonly large share of a market for a time, only to lose it. Many of those companies no longer exist. Perhaps it is only fair that the workers in such a company receive a share of these larger profits. But fairness would also seem to require that they be willing to share in some of the losses and sacrifices that often precede and follow the unpredictable periods of prosperity.

Many businessmen would not object to their employees participating in a profit-sharing plan. But it would seem fair to require that if the employees of a particular company want a guaranteed share of the profits, they should be willing to share some of the risks. Robert Nozick has addressed this question.[8] He notes that whatever the lot of the working class in the past may have been, many members of the working class today have access to cash reserves. Large cash reserves also exist in union pension funds. According to Nozick, the fact that large segments of the working force in America could invest "raises the question of why this money isn't used to establish worker-controlled factories. Why haven't radicals and social democrats urged this?"[9] If the reply is given that workers themselves "lack the entrepreneurial ability to identify promising opportunities for profitable activity, and to organize firms to respond to these opportunities," then why

don't the workers "hire entrepreneurs and managers
to start a firm for them and then turn the authority functions over to the workers (who are the
owners) after one year"?[10] Nozick thinks the reason is obvious.

It's risky starting a new firm. One can't
identify easily new entrepreneurial talent,
and much depends on estimates of future
demand and of availability of resources, on
unforeseen obstacles, on chance, and so
forth. Specialized investment institutions
and sources of venture capital develop to run
just these risks. Some persons don't want to
run these risks of investing or backing new
ventures, or starting ventures themselves.
Capitalist society allows the separation of
the bearing of these risks from other activities. The workers in the Edsel branch of the
Ford Motor Company did not bear the risks of
the venture. In a socialist society, either
one must share in the risks of the enterprise
one works in, or everybody shares in the
risks of the investment decisions of the central investment managers. There is no way to
divest oneself of these risks or to choose to
carry some such risks but not others...as one
can do in a capitalist society.[11]

Nozick points out how often some people who
are unwilling to assume risks "feel entitled to
rewards from those who do and win; yet these same
people do not feel obligated to help out by shar-
ing the losses of those who bear risks and lose."[12]
He asks, "Why do some feel they may stand back to
see whose ventures turn out well...and then claim
a share of the success; though they do not feel
they must bear the losses if things turn out
poorly, or feel that if they wish to share in the
profits or the control of the enterprise, they
should invest and run the risks also?"[13] Capitalism affords a significant advantage to those people who would shift the risks to others and who
prefer the security of a fixed income. They can
have the security they want. But they should not

begrudge the individual who shouldered the risk
any profit he might be fortunate enough to receive
from his investment.

In summary, the argument that capitalism is
immoral because it necessarily exploits the worker
by allowing the capitalist excess profits at the
worker's expense is a mixed bag. It is perfectly
consistent with a market system to defuse this
possibility by offering the workers a chance to
share in all "excess profits," whatever this might
be taken to mean. But why should workers be given
an opportunity to share any winnings without also
bearing an equal responsibility to share the risks
and possible losses? Thus, it is clearly false
that capitalism necessarily involves the exploitation of the worker.

3. Capitalism is immoral because it leads to
the exploitation of underdeveloped countries.
Something like this is usually meant whenever capitalism is equated with imperialism. Richard T.
DeGorge points out the weakness of this charge.

Industrial countries today still import raw
materials from other countries which are sometimes less developed. This fact by itself
does not equal exploitation. Moreover, the
raw materials can be sold to countries run more
or less on the capitalistic model or to countries run on the socialistic model. The price
at which the material is sold does not depend
on the economic system of the buyer country.
Hence, the case cannot be sustained that the
capitalistic countries depend on exploitation
unless the socialistic countries are to be
blamed likewise. The evil, in that case, would
not be an evil of capitalism, but an evil of
well-to-do or industrial as opposed to poor
and non-industrial countries.[14]

Countries that take advantage of weaker nations
are those that are richer, more powerful or more
industrialized. But these advantages are exercised by socialist nations as well as nations that

approximate a market economy. The claim that capitalism necessarily involves the exploitation of weaker and poorer nations can only be made by those who ignore the equal complicity of socialist States. The argument is another example of the Fallacy of False Cause. It presumes that because nation A exploited nation B, and because A approximated a free economy, it was nation A's capitalism that caused the exploitation. This reasoning ignores the other features of A (possible militarism, power, wealth, etc.) that are more likely causes, especially since these other features are also found in socialist States that practice exploitation.

4. Capitalism is immoral because it panders to greed and selfishness. According to William Coates, "In a capitalist society the primary virtues are competitiveness, greed and ambition. These virtues, it is said, provide the necessary energy which motivates the whole system."[15] The claim that the market panders to human greed is false. A proper understanding of the operation of the market will show how the market, in fact, neutralizes greed. One may lust after the property of another all he wants. But as long as the rights of the second party are protected, the greed of the first individual cannot harm him. So long as the first person is prohibited from using force, theft or fraud, his greed for another's property must be channeled into the discovery of products or services for which people are willing to exchange their own holdings. Greed can never harm another person so long as his rights are protected. If Mr. X is going to satisfy his greed within a market system of rights, he is going to have to offer others something that they want in exchange. His greed must lead him to a product or service which others are willing to barter for. Thus, every person in the market has to be other-directed. Each must ask himself what other people want and how he can best service those wants. Therefore, any greed that might operate in the market involves a paradox. The market is one area of life where concern for the other person is

required. The market, then, does not pander to
greed. It is rather a mechanism that allows natural human desires to be satisfied in a non-
violent way. The alternative to free exchange is
violence.

The market is an instrument that enables people to attain individual goals in a voluntary,
non-violent way. It is difficult to see how the
pursuit of individual goals, which the market
makes possible, is equivalent to selfishness. It
requires a great deal of question-begging to
equate even the pursuit of monetary profit with
selfishness. Since profit can be a means to other
ends, it can be used for selfish or for altruistic
purposes. The market only reflects the values of
the people who use it. The pursuit of goals, even
profits, is not selfish per se. Moreover, the
needy members of a society cannot be helped by the
productive members until the economic system produces at least enough to go around. The free market makes private and public charity possible in
this way. No competitive economic system can
match the market's record of productivity.

5. _Capitalism is immoral because it inevitably produces situations in which some people gain
at the expense of others_. Objections like this
assume that capitalism is exploitative in the
sense that the seller always takes unfair advantage of the buyer, that he _uses_ the buyer, in some
sense. The assumption is that some competitive
economic system, socialism presumably, would create a climate in which buyers and sellers would
become much more considerate of each other. This
charge is clearly based on a false analogy. When
two people play checkers, it is true that only one
of them can win. But it is a mistake to assume
that because the entrepreneur has made a profit,
he has won and the buyer has lost. On the contrary, the market is one place where one person's
gain need _not_ be another's loss. The market is
one place where both parties can win. It is just
as true that the seller _uses_ the buyer. In the
market, exchanges occur when both parties get

168

something they wanted. Unless both parties to an exchange were satisfied, they would not have bothered. Whether the exchange really was mutually beneficial is beside the point; it took place because both sides believed it was beneficial. As long as force and fraud are excluded from economic exchange, both parties can walk away as winners.

This analysis is pertinent to employer-employee relationships. Some people assume that the employer always wins at the expense of his employees. But in this form of market exchange, the employee is trading his time, effort, and labor for something else he wants more, his salary. Since he is getting something he wants, he is anything but a victim. This argument does not assume for one moment that all or even many such exchanges are idyllic. But the point is that there is nothing inherently exploitative in the exchange process. Now, of course, exchanges occasionally take place under conditions where someone does in fact lose. Because conditions may be unfavorable, a person may be forced to sell something at a time or for a price he finds inconvenient, while another person who can wait for more opportune circumstances may be able to make a profit. Under the wrong conditions, any buyer or seller might come away from a transaction as the loser. But even in such cases, the agent is moved by the belief that the exchange is preferable to some alternative. Nor does this argument ignore the problem of corruption within any system. Certainly there are dishonest employers; there are also dishonest employees who collect a full day's wages for less than a full day's work. The market is a tool that is used by both moral and immoral people. It hardly seems fair to blame it for the immoral practices of some without also praising it for the indispensable service it affords to moral people.

6. Capitalism is immoral because it encourages people to spend their money on trivial, useless, or immoral products. This popular objection to capitalism is often, for obvious reasons,

169

dubbed the Puritanical Argument. A free market, it claims, produces too many of the wrong goods. The market floods society with a surplus of trivial, worthless, and perhaps even dangerous items.

> The market for consumer goods is now characterized by the sale of more and more useless items. Those items that are still necessary are more and more laden with useless accessories, fringes, decorations and anything that can be used to increase the price. Thousands of virtually identical products--produced with enormous waste in duplication--compete for consumer's attention in supermarkets and department stores under different brand names. To make the system work, billions are spent on advertising to assure a customer's preference for one identical product over another.[16]

The proponent of the Puritanical Argument often omits an important part of his conclusion. Rothbard fills in the gaps: "If people are immoral enough to choose whiskey rather than milk, cosmetics rather than educational matter, then the State, they say, should step in and correct these choices."[17] The fact that improper choices of individual citizens will have to be corrected by the hopefully more intelligent decisions of bureaucratic elites arouses concern that the cure could be worse than the disease. The argument implies that

> consumers ought to be deprived of freedom of choice, and...government bureaucrats, full of wisdom...should make their consumptive choices for them. The consumers should be supplied, not with what they themselves want, but with what bureaucrats of exquisite taste and culture think is good for them. And the way to do this is to tax away from people all the income they have been foolish enough to earn above that required to meet their bare necessities, and turn it over to the bureaucrats to be spent in ways in which the latter

170

think would really do people the most good...
all supplied, of course, by government.[18]

But who will appoint the governmental elit-
ists who will make these decisions for the consumer? It would hardly be consistent for the
proponent of this argument to maintain that the
government should be elected democratically.
After all, if the people cannot be trusted to make
relatively minor economic decisions in their normal everyday affairs, how can they be trusted in
the much more important matter of recognizing
those qualified to lead them? If the power of
modern advertising is so irresistable that the
typical consumer cannot freely choose between
brands of breakfast cereal, his susceptibility to
persuasion certainly disqualifies him as a competent judge of political leadership. Rothbard has
a point when he suggests that "anyone who advocates governmental dictation over one area of
individual consumption must logically come to
advocate complete totalitarian dictation over all
choices."[19]

But aside from its sinister implications for
human liberty, how fair is the kind of reasoning
found in the Puritanical Argument? Imagine an
individual who visits a particular restaurant so
frequently and eats so gluttonously that he gains
thirty pounds in just a few weeks. Suppose one
day that the now badly overweight gentleman begins
to berate his regular waiter for his corpulence.
Who really is at fault? All the waiter did was
bring the meals that the customer ordered. That
was his job. The real fault obviously rests with
the diner. In a similar way, the advocate of the
Puritanical Argument blames the market for the
mistakes of the consumers. If an economic system
permits the consumer to make free choices, it can
hardly be blamed if the consumer chooses unwisely.
Surely the consumer has to bear much of the
responsibility for trivial or poor quality goods.
One might question the ethics of the businessman
who produces a poorer quality product for a lower
price. But if the consumer is willing to pay the

171

price of lower quality in trade for lower cost, should he not have that privilege? The obvious rebuttal to the Puritanical Argument is that "the market economy is simply a resultant of individual valuations, and thus...the fault lies with the valuations, not the economic system."20

The claim that all bad habits and bad tastes of consumers are caused by wicked producers is equally suspect.

The philosophy is not only based on the doctrine depicting the common people as guileless suckers who can easily be taken in by the ruses of a race of crafty hucksters. It implies in addition the nonsensical theorem that the sale of articles which the consumer really needs and would buy if not hypnotized by the wiles of the sellers is unprofitable for business and that on the other hand only the sale of articles which are of little or no use for the buyer or are even downright detrimental to him yields large profits.[21]

The irony of statists who bemoan the consumer's lack of free choice under a market economy and then urge that all economic choices be turned over to a central planning committee should not be overlooked. The inconsistency is so obvious as to appear hypocritical. Even though consumers under a market economy are open to persuasion from a variety of sources including parents, friends, as well as advertisers, they still make choices among a variety of enticements. If this were not true, it would be impossible to account for the existence of so many competing advertisements. The power of consumers to choose freely, and by those choices influence future offerings of the market, is far greater under capitalism than under the centralized planning desired by the critics of the market.

The charge of planned obsolescence that usually accompanies the Puritanical Argument is clearly incompatible with the evidence. If manufacturers really did design products that quickly fell apart, foreign competition and consumer resentment would soon drive them out of business. What the enemy of the market sees as planned obsolescence is frequently continued improvement of new products that does indeed produce dissatisfaction with the older and now inferior product. The old Ford Model T was profitable for years at the same time that it avoided planned obsolescence. But Ford was eventually compelled to change its design by the consumer's desire for a new and better product. Competition in the tire industry has produced remarkable advances in the product. Only competition would have worked so successfully in producing this search for improvement. Would a state-owned monopoly unchallenged by any competitor have had much incentive to improve its product? More than likely, a government-run industry would have remained content with the old product.

7. Capitalism is immoral because it depends upon the morally questionable practice of advertising which creates artificial need, manipulates people, and debases taste. The economist, Israel Kirzner, notes how "Advertising, a pervasive feature of the market economy, is widely misunderstood and often condemned as wasteful, inefficient, inimical to competition, and generally destructive of consumer sovereignty."[22] Complaints about the questionable ethics and bad taste of much contemporary advertising strike a raw nerve with many reflective people. Clearly, what often passes for advertising is less than honorable or uplifting. But on the other hand, it is important to recognize the essential function advertising serves in a free society. It is a vital source of information for the buyer, alerting him to new products or new opportunities. The charge that advertising unfairly passes along an unnecessary cost to the consumer results from a failure to grasp an important fact about production costs. Kirzner explains that it

might seem that the entrepreneur's function
is fulfilled when he transforms an opportunity to produce a potential product into an
opportunity for the consumer to buy the
finished product. Consumers themselves were
not aware of the opportunities this production process represents; it is the superior
alertness of the entrepreneur that has
enabled him to fulfill his task. It is not
sufficient, however, to make the product
available; consumers must be aware of its
availability. If the opportunity to buy is
not perceived by the consumer, it is as if
the opportunity to produce has not been perceived by the entrepreneur. It is not enough
to grow food consumers do not know how to
obtain; consumers must know that the food has
in fact been grown! Providing consumers with
information is not enough. It is essential
that the opportunities available to the consumer attract his attention, whatever the
degree of his alertness may be. Not only
must the entrepreneur-producer marshall
resources to cater to consumer desires, but
also he must insure that the consumer does
not miss what has been wrought. For this
purpose advertising is clearly an indispensable instrument.[23]

Kirzner is clearly correct when he concludes, "All
costs are in the last analysis selling costs."[24]

Advertising also insures accessibility to
markets by new and thus relatively unknown sellers. Thanks to advertising, it is easier for new
sellers to gain entry to the market.[25] It is
untrue that advertising increases the cost of the
product, a cost that must be absorbed by the victimized consumer. Advertising usually reduces
price.[26] Advertising should be viewed as one sign
of the entrepreneur's basic insecurity. Every
day, when he opens for business, he lacks sufficient information to tell him what will happen.
He is at the mercy of an innumerable number of
unknown factors. If he's lucky and guesses right,

174

he can make a profit. If he's unlucky or guesses
wrong, he will lose. He can never be sure what
the market will do to him today. Consequently,
the advertiser is trying to allay his fears and
draw the consumer's attention to his product or
service. While we may not like the form his
advertising takes, it is an indispensable part of
a free market. The questionable values frequently
observed in some types of advertising reflect as
much on the standards of the potential customer as
on the character of the advertiser. If that kind
of advertising did not work, it would not be used.
Harold Demsetz notes ironically that "intellectuals, so dedicated to the principle of free
speech that they actively defend pornography, can
hardly object to advertising because commercials
are done poorly."27

Philip Nelson summarizes the problem of
advertising nicely.

> In summary, while advertising is not
> exactly a shiny white knight distributing
> Ajax as it gallops, it is not evil incarnate.
> On average, advertising is doing a good job,
> making an important contribution to the
> information of consumers and the competitive
> operation of markets.
> But advertising is an institution that can
> be improved. Unfortunately, most of the pro-
> posals that have been made to improve upon
> advertising would make matters worse. Basi-
> cally, these reforms are flawed by a failure
> to understand how advertising works. As in
> most economic problems, a 'good heart' is
> insufficient equipment to produce a better
> world.28

Thus, while advertising is indeed an essential
part of a free market system, claims that it is a
morally questionable or taste-debasing practice
are guilty of blaming a legitimate practice
because of its misuse by some. The same reasoning
would abolish the practice of medicine because
some use it corruptly.

8. **Capitalism is immoral because of its inability to provide basic public goods that are not clearly profitable.** John Arthur and William Shaw articulate this charge by arguing that "the market mechanism cannot provide certain goods which are in everyone's interest--a decent urban environment, pollution-free air, public transportation, parks--goods which lack an attractive profit angle."[29] In a similar vein, Norman Bowie and Robert Simon maintain that the

> market mechanism does not apply to certain goods--most of them in the public sector. For private goods, my consumption affects your consumption. You cannot eat the apple that I have eaten. For this reason each of us will express our true desires for the apple in the market place. The price one is willing to pay is a measurement of that desire. Hence, the pricing mechanism rations scare goods according to one's willingness to pay. Regrettably, this rationing scheme does not work for public goods. You can drive on the same road that I drive on. Hence, when it comes time to fix the road, you will understate the price you are willing to pay, hoping that I will pick up the burden. Of course, as rational egoists we all think this way, and the real value of the road to use is not reflected in the market place as is the real value of the apples.[30]

In other words, capitalism's great efficiency in meeting private needs where profits can be made is not duplicated in cases of public needs that provide little opportunity for profit. In fact, capitalism is notoriously inefficient in such cases.

Clearly, this line of argument applies only to extreme Libertarians or anarcho-capitalists who reject entirely any role for the State. But this option has already been eliminated. Most defenders of the market admit the possibility of some public goods that may require state-action for

176

their implementation. Milton Friedman, for example, acknowledges that we may "want to do through government some things that might conceivably be done through the market but that technical or similar conditions render it difficult to do in that way. These all reduce to cases in which strictly voluntary exchange is either exceedingly costly or practically impossible."31 This would certainly be true in the case of "general access roads, involving many points of entry and exit [where] the costs of collection would be extremely high if a charge were to be made for the specific services received from each individual...."32 Defenders of the market like Friedman insist, however, that the scope of such public goods is much smaller than is usually believed. For example, the provision of a quality education probably requires funding through taxation. But as Friedman has shown, it does not require public school systems. The quality of education would be greatly increased if schools actually had to compete for pupils on a free and open market. Friedman suggests that the State return tax-money to parents in the form of vouchers which the parents could use to pay for their children's education at any school they chose. The ensuing competition would quickly result in poorer quality schools being driven out of the educational market.33 Present federal policies that obscure the true costs of public goods to those who benefit from them are unfair. For example, people who use public transportation in New York City should pay the full costs of the system. Under present policies of the federal government, the losses of the New York system are subsidized by taxpayers in the rest of the country whose federal tax dollars are channeled to the municipal government of New York City. The nature of such hidden costs lessens the incentive of politicians to hold down costs.

The objection against capitalism appears clearly irrelevant because few defenders of the market deny the existence of all public goods. The statist's argument diverts attention from the more serious ethical implications of continual expansions of the sphere of these allegedly public goods. Present tax policies that disguise the true costs of many "services" should be abandoned.

9. <u>Capitalism is immoral because the pursuit of profit frequently results in serious side effects, the cost of which is unfairly passed along to people who should not have to pay</u>. The environmental crisis has shown that the consumption and production of many goods and services can produce serious side effects. If the things that are presently polluted like air and water were property, no one would be <u>free</u> to use them as garbage dumps. That is not to say these things would cease to be polluted; it is to recognize that people could not pollute them <u>freely</u>, that is, without being obliged to pay the costs of pollution. According to David (not Milton) Friedman, "If the pollution were done to something that belonged to someone, the owner would permit it only if the pollutor were willing to pay him more than the damage done. If the pollutors themselves owned the property they were polluting, it would pay them to stop if the damage they did were greater than the cost of avoiding it; few of us want to dump our garbage on our own front lawns."34

Short of terminating the entire human race, there is no way to end pollution. Even then, non-human life would continue the process of pollution to some extent. The point to the pollution problem is to insure that the damage done remains less than what it would cost to avoid the pollution. But who should pay for reducing or eliminating the pollutants? Two companies manufacturing the same product might both produce the same amount of air pollution. As long as both accepted the cost of reducing the pollution and passed the cost on to the consumer in the form of a higher price, the problem could be eased. But if only one company treated pollution as an internalized cost, its product would be more expensive than that of the free-loading company which would then gain a distinct market advantage. One way to

handle this is to assign property rights to the
air that is polluted. This would require any
company polluting the air to pay a price high
enough to compensate the owner of that property
right for the poorer quality of air. However, the
problems of converting something like air into
property where individual property rights can be
easily identified are too obvious to mention. One
solution is to admit a limited role to the State
and assign these property rights to the government.

If pollution control is to be handled by
government, it should be done by [letting]
the government set a price, per cubic foot of
each pollutant, for polluting. Such a price
might vary according to where the pollution
is created; air pollution in Manhattan presumably does more damage than in the Mojave
desert. Every pollutor, from the United
States Steel Corporation down to the individual motorist, would have to pay. If the cost
of avoiding pollution is really high, the
firm will continue to pollute--and pay for
it. Otherwise, it will stop. If the voters
think there is still too much pollution, they
can vote to raise the price; it is a relatively simple issue.... If pollutors must pay
for their pollution, however avoidable or
unavoidable, we will rapidly find out which
ones can or cannot stop polluting.[35]

Two final observations are in order. Critics
of technology seldom combine their criticism of
the products of technology with their own willing-
ness to forsake the advantages of technology.
Many take full advantage of their society's technology and then hypocritically denounce the by-
products of the technology from which they benefit.
Moreover, it is important to challenge the simplistic assumption that whenever imperfections
show up in the market, intervention by the State
is necessary. Seldom is this assumption supported
with evidence that the government will do a better

179

job. Considerable evidence exists that governments do a worse job.

10. Capitalism is immoral because it causes human alienation. Karl Marx, utilizing insights borrowed from the philosophy of Hegel, first made this charge in some of his early manuscripts which were written several years before The Communist Manifesto.[36] Marx believed that capitalism causes worker alienation in several ways. First, the worker is alienated from that which he produces. Marcuse was simply echoing this view when he claimed that the worker becomes dominated and controlled by the things created by the economic system. Secondly, the worker is estranged from the labor process itself. No great effort is required to note how many men and women hate their jobs. This alienation from one's work is not restricted to those who must labor at menial, repetitive, boring, dirty, or degrading occupations. Even professional golfers and philosophers have been known to hold an occasional loathing for their job. Thirdly, the worker under capitalism becomes alienated from other men, a fact easily observed by attending to the widespread competitiveness, hostility, and animosity among human beings. And finally, the poor worker even becomes alienated from himself. Surely, writes DeGeorge on behalf of those persuaded by this argument, "There is something wrong with a society that values goods more than people, that dehumanizes people in the labor process, and that fragments human beings into competitors, preventing them from social cooperation and mutual respect."[37]

The evidence suggests that all of the forms of alienation noted by Marx exist under capitalism. But surely such alienation is not a feature of capitalist societies alone. As DeGeorge indicates,

in those societies in which the private ownership of the means of production has been done away with, there is no perceptible decline in alienation, in the desire for

goods, in the dehumanization that is toler-
ated in factories, and so on. And in
societies which continue to have private
ownership of the means of production, we find
growing numbers less interested in goods than
their parents; we find a stronger defense of
human rights than elsewhere; we find a consciousness that certain types of work can be
dehumanizing and stultifying and attempts to
change such conditions; and we find not only
competition but also cooperation and a will-
ingness to work together.[38]

It is difficult to believe that a garbage collector in Moscow is any happier with his job than a
garbage collector in Boston. Alienation and
dehumanization are serious problems, but it is
simply not true that they result only from conditions existing in capitalist societies and vanish
once societies have become socialist.

THE ALLEGED IRRATIONALISM OF CAPITALISM

Capitalism is alleged to suffer from a number
of internal contradictions that make its eventual
self-destruction inevitable. The first of these
is: 1. Capitalism is irrational because it leads
inevitably to drastic irregularities in economic
cycles. Enemies of the free market object to it
on grounds of its inherent tendency to produce
boom-or-bust cycles. A market economy is supposed
to be notoriously unstable.

Even when it is performing at its best,
capitalism is subject to booms and busts
which take a frightful human toll in terms
of insecurity and enforced idleness. At
other times, as during the 1930's and to an
increasing extent in the last few years, a
condition of chronic stagnation and continuing mass unemployment is superimposed upon
the normal ups and downs of the system.[39]

181

The market's alleged instability is used as
grounds for justifying the need for the State to
take over the reins of the economy. Murray Rothbard draws attention to the frequency with which
the Great Depression is cited as proof of the
instability of the free market.

> The chief impact of the Great Depression
> on American thought was universal acceptance
> of the view that 'laissez-faire capitalism'
> was to blame. The common opinion--among
> economists and the lay public alike--holds
> that 'Unreconstructed Capitalism' prevailed
> during the 1920's, and that the tragic
> depression shows that old-fashioned laissez-
> faire can work no longer.... The government
> must step in to stablilize the economy and
> iron out the business cycle. A vast army of
> people to this day consider capitalism almost
> permanently on trial. If the modern array of
> monetary-fiscal management and stabilizers
> cannot save capitalism from another severe
> depression, this large group will turn to
> socialism as the final answer....40

However, Rothbard counters, this common wisdom about the causes of the Great Depression must
not be allowed to pass unchallenged. It rests, he
insists, on the unproven "assumption that business
cycles in general, and depressions in particular,
arise from the depths of the free-market, capitalist economy." This assumption, he contends, "is
pure myth, resting not on proof but on simple
faith."41 The truth is actually to be found in a
competing economic tradition. As Rothbard
explains, this competing "view holds that business
cycles and depressions stem from disturbances gen-
erated in the market by monetary intervention.
The monetary theory holds that money and credit-
expansion, launched by the banking system, causes
booms and busts."42 Interventionists love to
claim that the Great Depression resulted from a
basic flaw in capitalism and that only statist
intervention adjusted the economy back to a sta-
ble position. Rothbard's book shows that the

182

situation prior to the Great Depression was anything but a period of unbridled <u>laissez-faire</u>.
The Depression resulted not from some defect
intrinsic to a market economy, but from government
mismanagement before, during, and after the economic collapse of 1929. What made matters worse
and turned what would have been an otherwise moderate economic contraction (caused, of course, by
prior governmental mismanagement) into a major
disaster was an improper monetary policy adopted
by the Federal Reserve System between 1930-1931.
Roosevelt's New Deal was simply an example of
additional intervention being called upon to prop
up the failures of Herbert Hoover's earlier interventionist policies.

Periodic oscillations of prosperity and
depression that critics of the market believe are
endemic to capitalism are, in fact, a consequence
of a fractional-reserve gold standard, especially
one that exists "with a central bank, a government
and a public opinion eager to keep expanding credit to start a 'full employment' boom or to keep
it going...."[43] As Henry Hazlitt explains, business cycles are caused by monetary and credit
expansion.

> The credit expansion does not raise all
> prices simultaneously and uniformly. Tempted
> by the deceptively low interest rates it
> initially brings about, the producers of
> capital goods borrow the money for new-long
> term projects. This leads to distortions in
> the economy. It leads to overexpansion in
> the production of capital goods, and to other
> malinvestments that are only recognized as
> such after the boom has been going on for a
> considerable time. When this malinvestment
> does not become evident, the boom collapses.
> The whole economy and structure of production
> must undergo a painful readjustment accom-
> panied by greatly increased unemployment.[44]

Therefore, the reply of the free market to this
critique of the market is that the kind of

instability under discussion is not an inherent feature of the market. It results instead from governmental intervention with the market process that interrupts the market's informational function. For example, in a free market, low interest rates indicate that money is plentiful and that prospects for long range investment are favorable. High interest rates indicate a shortage of money and suggest the need for pessimism and caution. Interventionist policies that artificially alter the money supply and interest rates shut off this information. The major American depressions that occured in 1837, 1873, 1892, and 1929 were all

> preceded by several years of government-inspired inflation of one kind or another.... There were other factors in these boom-and-bust cycles, but in each case the central ingredient has been credit expansion resulting from some form of government intervention. This is not to say that business fluctuations would not take place otherwise, for business-men will often guess wrong, make mistakes, and will invest too deeply in the wrong place at the wrong time. But the effect will be local and short-lived. With the inexorable push of deliberate government policy, the entire economy usually finds itself swept along on a nation-wide wave of speculation that builds higher and higher and then collapses.[45]

Therefore, this particular attack on the market is a classic example of the market being blamed for the disastrous consequences of interventionist policies. The argument should actually be applied to economic interventionism.

2. <u>Capitalism is irrational because it leads to the establishment of monopolies.</u> In the view of those who advance this objection, capitalism is promoted on the premise that maximum competition will insure the perfect operation of the market whereas, in fact, the free market system encourages the increased consolidation of power and capital into a few firms that gain effective

monopolistic control. The very system that promotes competition leads to a destruction of competition. This kind of reasoning often assumes that larger firms gain such unfair advantage over smaller or less successful firms that prospective competitors find it impossible to gain effective access to the market while older and weaker competitors are driven out of business or absorbed in mergers. Once immunity from competition is attained, the argument continues, producers lose any incentive to produce the best products at the lowest price. Such domination of a market would make de facto price-fixing possible.

The first thing the proponent of this argument needs to do is present a clear and defensible definition of "monopoly." As things turn out, this is not as easy as it might seem. The term is usually used to refer to any person or business that gains the position of being the single seller of some product. But this definition doesn't help at all. The use of "monopoly" in this way makes Robinson Crusoe and his friend, Friday, into monopolists, since each was the single seller on their island of lumber and fish. But what precisely was so wicked about the exclusiveness that each man had with respect to his particular product? Rothbard asks, "if Crusoe and Friday are not wicked, how can a more complex society, one necessarily less monopolistic in this sense, be at all wicked?"46 After all, the products the contemporary "monopolist" markets are not homogeneous products like fish or lumber. The car the General Motors sells is a composite of thousands of parts, supplied by many different sources. "At what point in the reduced scope of such monopoly can it be considered evil? And how can the market be held responsible for the number of people inhabiting the society?"47 Until defenders of the monopolistic-argument come up with a clear and defensible meaning for "monopoly," the credibility of their claim must be suspect.

The monopolistic-argument ignores evidence that shows how difficult it is to achieve actual

185

control over a total market. While the Ralston Purina Company is perhaps the most successful company in the animal food market, it has been unable to extend that success into the human cereal market. Similarly, General Mills, an admittedly powerful force in the human cereal market, has been generally ineffectual in translating its manufacturing and marketing expertise into the animal food market.

Much of the plausibility of the monopolistic-argument depends upon a false picture of the market. It is surprising how many friends and enemies of the market persist in the thought that capitalism requires some kind of perfect competition. This model, a hang-over from classical economics, is fallacious.

Contrary to the way the market is defined by many, it is <u>not</u> the classical economic model where there are many sellers and many buyers. Rather...the market is simply what results from the free choices made by individuals without government interference. Indeed, the simple 'many buyers/many sellers' ideal is recognized by supporters of the market as static and without much choice or innovation while the market is actually dynamic and most complex and without any predetermined form.48

Textbook models of perfect competition often suggest a "tendency for price to gravitate toward the equilibrium level at which quantity demanded equals quantity supplied."49 But economists of the Austrian School like Von Mises, Hayek, Kirzner, and Rothbard reject the <u>static</u> view of the market that accompanies the notion of equilibrium. They offer instead a <u>dynamic</u> model. For them, the market is constantly in a state of process. Disequilibrium in the market "occurs precisely because market participants do not know what the market-clearing price is."50 Because the defense of the free market does not require any notion of perfect competition, the inability of

186

economists to discover such in the market counts as a mark only against a faulty economic model and not against the market itself. Static views of the market naturally encourage a misguided pessimism about the market's tendency to encourage the concentration of power and capital. In reality, the market is a process of creative destruction with competing forces attempting and often succeeding in wiping out the opposition.

Abandonment of the static view of the market suggests still another point relevant to the monopolistic-argument. The dynamic view of the market "sees competition as multiple and complex, where products compete on many bases (price only being one) with all other products, actual and potential."[51] In other words, even if one firm could, for a time, gain dominance of the merchandising of a particular commodity, it would still have to compete with the merchandisers of every other commodity for the consumer's money. If people spend their money on a new dress or suit, they no longer have that money to spend for a theater ticket or a restaurant meal or a new book or gasoline. The scarcity of commodities and money forces the consumer to make an unending series of choices based upon his particular valuations at the time. Once those choices are made, that money is no longer available for other choices. In this kind of complex economic environment, no businessman can effectively control his customers. The car manufacturer is not simply competing against other car makers; he is competing with every other merchant of every other product. General Motors' present domination of the American automobile market won't mean a thing if enough consumers decide to forego the purchase of a new car for other commodities that they, at the time, value more highly.

It is widely believed that recent decades have seen an increase in the number of business failings as more and more power becomes concentrated in fewer companies. Donald Devine cites the statistics that show how false this belief is.

The evidence shows very little change in the rate of business failures.[52] Of course, Devine admits, plenty of evidence exists to show how political interference with the market (tariffs, regulations, subsidies, etc.) has the effect of offsetting market operations. But, he adds,

> to the degree that the market is unfettered it appears that managers face restraints upon the wealth they nominally control.... If the market were as weak as critics suggest, it would seem that large corporations should at least be able to protect themselves from its forces. Yet there appears to be no positive correlation between concentration and lack of competition. Even some of the largest firms fail in the market.... When allowed to operate, though, the market buffets corporations and subjects them to its discipline. Even the most minimal theory of concentration--that a large corporation can hold its market position over time--does not stand up.[53]

The belief that capitalism breeds monopoly is contradicted by the evidence. The only real monopolies that have ever attained total immunity from competition achieved that status by governmental fiat, regulation, or support of some other kind. Governments create monopolies by granting one organization the exclusive privilege of doing business or by establishing de facto monopolies through regulatory agencies whose alleged purpose is the enforcement of competition.[54] The only monopolies that pose a challenge to market principles are those that result from statist interference with the market.

3. Capitalism is irrational because it contains within itself the seeds of its own destruction. This self-destruction is supposed to occur because capitalism leads to overproduction that makes economic disaster inevitable. William L. Baker summarizes this Marxist view:

188

Capitalism, then, dies of gluttony. More correctly, capitalistic society dies of hunger induced by indigestion.... Production [under capitalism] was nothing other than a juggernaut relentlessly crushing everything in its path. Trade and prosperity were nothing else but the dormant seeds of a future crash. The only refuge from poverty (the effects of the crash) was to abstain from production and trade. In a word, the only refuge from poverty is poverty itself.[55]

Marx's analysis of the inevitable collapse of capitalism assumed that the capitalist's obsession with profit would lead him continually to expand production and reduce costs. His reduction of costs would entail paying his workers as little as possible. But the continued production would produce an oversupply of goods which the impoverished, victimized, and exploited workers would be unable to afford. Thus the capitalist's mad rush to profit will end in a glutted market. The fact that an insufficient number of consumers have the resources to afford his products is also his fault. Eventually, this house of cards must collapse.

Marx's "analysis" presumes an almost unbelievable stupidity on the part of the capitalist. If an employer has any sense at all, he will want to get the maximum productivity from his workers. If they are not paid enough to eat well and stay healthy, if they are not paid enough to remain motivated, the businessman deserves exactly what he will get. Even if a businessman lacks one grain of altruism, an enlightened self-interest should tell him that the well-being of his employees is important to his own survival. Marx also assumed that capitalists were incapable of learning from past mistakes of overproduction, that an incredible collection of errors would all be made at the same time, and that industrialists would persist in continuing production even when no one was able to purchase their products.

How and why, with bulging inventories of
unpurchased goods, would assembly belts continue to roll? Continued production under
such circumstances would be suicidal and
impossible. But capitalists are neither
suicidal, overly charitable, nor infinitely
rich. The Marxist sees the entrepreneur (or
capitalist), however, as a total nitwit,
completely unable to adapt to changing circumstances. And whatever else might be said
of the industrialist magnate, he is not lacking in versatility. How could such a condition (overproduction) exist outside the
realm of fairy tales and propaganda pam-
phlets? The law of scarcity has never been
repealed. The tissue of fallacies must be
faced: the theory of overproduction is long
overdue for a well-deserved rest.56

Once again, a frequently cited.objection to the
market appears plausible only because someone has
stacked the deck. The myth of overproduction is
a straw man.

　　　4. Capitalism is irrational because of its
erroneous assumption that consumers are rational
creatures who will always seek the maximum satisfaction of their wants in a rational and predictable manner. But, the critic counters, consumers
are notoriously irrational. They are frequently
moved by habit, instinct, tradition or other nonrational influences to act in ways quite contrary
to how a rational person in the market should
behave. Consequently, the market is not the
rational system its defenders believe it to be.
For example, executives in the McDonald's organization might reasonably expect that their success
in selling hamburgers in America and England can
be easily repeated in any other country. This
expectation would receive a rude shock, however,
were they to attempt to sell hamburgers in
Calcutta, India. Consumers do fail to behave in
ways that someone obsessed by the rationality-
thesis might expect. People often pay higher
prices for products because of habit (they have

always done business with a particular merchant)
or convenience (the store is in their neighborhood) or some other reason. Consumers are notoriously fickle and unpredictable. If they were
not, only businesses run by nitwits would ever
fail.

Perhaps the most surprising thing about this
argument is the fact that anyone seriously
believes it applies to free market economics.
The school of Austrian Economics has sought for
decades to counter models of the market that view
it as an arena of rational satisfaction-
maximizers. Austrian economists like Von Mises,
Hayek, and Rothbard are correct in viewing economic value as purely subjective.[57] They are
right in repudiating the notion that the economic
value of anything is in some sense objective,
i.e., inherent in the object. Because the economic value people place upon things is completely
subjective, it is impossible to predict what people will value, why they will value it, and when
their priorities might change. The economist can
tell what people happen to value at the moment by
their actions on the market. But past performance
can never be a guarantee of future action. Consequently, this particular challenge to the free
market rests, like many others, on a distorted
model of how the market actually functions.

   5. Capitalism is irrational because of its
drastic inefficiencies that frequently result in
high unemployment. John Maynard Keynes is supposed, by interventionist economists, to have
shown the inefficiency of an unregulated market.
As Arthur and Shaw explain, "Equilibrium in a
free-market system, can, in fact be reached at a
less than optimal utilization of resources--at,
for example a high rate of unemployment. Consequently, the market cannot be relied upon to
eliminate poverty. Government intervention is
necessary to accomplish this...."[58] According to
Bowie and Simon, who agree, the mechanism of the
market can

be stuck on a lower rung of the economic ladder. The ideal is to have equilibrium at or
near full employment. However, Keynes showed
that the self-regulating features of the market were not sufficient to guarantee equilibrium at this ideal position. The market
can be in equilibrium at any level of
employment.[59]

The argument commits several errors. One
mistake, already noted, insists on applying the
outmoded and false analogy of equilibrium to the
free market. Attention has already been drawn to
the distorted picture that results from this
static view. The market is an on-going process
that never approaches some kind of static equilibrium.

The argument is aided considerably by a false
and misleading notion of what constitutes "full
employment." Most often, this phrase is taken to
mean a situation where everyone (or nearly everyone) has a job. This will never do. For one
thing, the job market is a constantly changing
process in which people continually enter and
leave the job force. It is far more accurate to
define "full employemnt" as a situation in which
everyone who is willing and able to work at the
prevailing wage rate is able to find a job.
Suppose Mr. Jones announces that he will refuse
any job that pays less than $50,000 a year.
Should he be included in the unemployment statistics? Suppose Mr. Smith refuses any job that
burns up more than 1000 calories in eight hours.
Should he be counted? Under present statistical
methods, both Jones and Smith would be counted as
unemployed. Surely, something is wrong here.

The group of unemployed workers always
includes four classes of people. (1) It includes
new entrants to the job market such as high school
graduates looking for their first full-time job.
But if Miss Hale and Mr. Hearty declare themselves
new entrants on June 1, why should they be immediately included within the ranks of the

192

unemployed? (2) The second class of unemployed are those who have recently quit their old job. Their present unemployment is a result of their free choice. They could have remained employed, had they wished. Should their present lack of employment be laid at the door of the free market system? (3) The third class would be those who have been recently fired. The job vacated because of their slothfulness or poor performance was immediately filled by someone else. (4) The final class of those without jobs are those who through no fault of their own were laid off as a result of their employer's declining business. There is good reason to regard this last class as the only group that should be counted as unemployed. Of course, comparatively few people remain unemployed for very long. The unemployment statistics suggest a picture of a huge army of victimized people totally unable to find work. The truth is that the statistics actually count people on their way to new employment, a situation which in three classes out of four, can hardly be blamed on the market. Why should the market be faulted for new entrants, re-entrants, and job quitters? At any given time, the actual percentage of truly unemployed people among all those not working is a comparatively small percentage of the total. Even in the case of this last group, Rothbard notes, "Unemployment is caused by unions or government keeping wage rates above the free-market level."[60] When forces like unions and the State do not artificially raise wage rates higher than the current market, the market will do a remarkably effective job of providing employment for those willing to work at the market-rate. Of course, this claim will not satisfy the critic of the market because he will then retreat to other arguments already answered, viz., that capitalists exploit the worker by paying unfairly low wages. This might be a good time to turn back to the beginning of this chapter and read it again.

CONCLUSION

The case against capitalism made on moral or rational grounds certainly appears less than overwhelming. What then accounts for the wide-spread and stubborn opposition to the system, even among those it has benefited the most? Perhaps more attention needs to be given to the irrational nature of much resistance to the market. Ernest Van Den Haag urges defenders of the market to "ask why their arguments have so little influence, why the policies they oppose continue, why the ideas they show to be wrong continue their hold on so many people. Ostrichlike, economists tend to ignore the nonrational sources of hostility to the market system."[61] It is sheer folly, he continues, to attempt to "counter irrational ideologies with rational arguments...[and] act as though irrational pseudo-reasoning and chiliastic longings can be fought successfully by proper economic reasoning.... The attempt of economists to tutor the emotionally committed is as doomed to failure as the attempts of philosophers to tutor the insane."[62]

Several irrational prejudices probably underlie many attacks on the market. Kirzner suggests as one example, "resentments which can arise from frustrated ambitions, of the envy on the part of the intellectuals and the white collar workers of the good fortunes enjoyed by successful entrepreneurs."[63] Envy may also manifest itself as a suspicion on the part of the less fortunate classes that the unequal distribution of wealth must be due to some sinister activities on the part of the more fortunate.

James Burnham points to guilt as a likely affective state to explain the hostility of wealthy Liberals to the free market.[64] The same suggestion has been made by the psychiatrist, Peter Breggin, himself a former Liberal. Breggin has written candidly about how his own feelings of guilt played a role in his Liberal commitment. He acknowledges, "I felt very guilty about my

advantages, and often thought about ways to help
the disadvantaged classes."[65] Breggin goes on to
say:

> The advantaged liberal idealist feels that
> his luck is unfair or unjust. In his heart
> he wishes everyone to have as much good luck
> or good fortune as he had. Extremists among
> advantaged liberal idealists are willing to
> sacrifice all of their good fortune even if
> it won't do anyone any good at all. Such an
> idealist is willing to sacrifice himself
> merely to 'even the score' without advancing
> anyone's benefit.... To defend against his
> guilt, the advantaged liberal idealist devel-
> ops the identity of 'good guy with good
> intentions.' He thinks of himself as someone
> who 'means well.' .... This form of liberal-
> ism, as I lived it myself for many years, is
> not really a philosophy or a political ideol-
> ogy. It is a psychology of good intentions
> whose aim is not so much to bring about
> change in the outside world as it is to
> assuage guilt within the inner personal
> world.[66]

While others have suggested a possible role for
guilt in attacks against the free market system,
Breggin adds a somewhat novel twist:

> The righteousness of the advantaged lib-
> eral idealist smacks of religiosity, and
> indeed, the 'liberalism' of this person comes
> much closer to religion than to politics: He
> seeks through his liberal humanitarianism to
> find redemption for the sin of being born
> with unfair advantage. Unlike the tradi-
> tional Christian, his struggle is not with
> the temptation to enjoy sex, alcohol or
> secular philosophies. His temptation is to
> enjoy his undeserved advantages. But his
> struggle with this awful temptation is no
> less difficult than that of the religion-
> ist.[67]

Breggin's article goes on to provide an interesting example that provides powerful support for many of the contentions of this book. Breggin's parents were poor immigrants who, eighty, years ago, joined hundreds of thousands of others in one of America's large city ghettos. Eventually, his parents rose out of poverty to positions of leadership in the business community. Breggin was led to reflect on the differences between the kind of ghetto in which his parents lived at the turn of the century and ghetto life under The Great Society.

Prior to the welfare state, Breggin notes, the ghettos in America

> bustled with activity. On every corner, vendors sold their wares--everything from clothing to food. People went from house to house offering their services as carpenters, plumbers or electricians. Whole families including teenaged children found employment, and added to the sum of the family income. Wages were low but not so low that most families could not improve themselves vastly over their previous lot in life. Individuals saved and then started businesses on shoestrings, and built them into mighty stores and chains of stores. People lived in poverty, yes; conditions were often very difficult, yes; but the poverty was alive, and the ghetto was a gateway into the American way of life. As countless autobiographies have demonstrated, many people thrived in these ghettos, and as they strove to better themselves, they left the ghettos behind, making room for others to immigrate into the country and to restart the cycle of revitalizing themselves and their new country.[68]

But those ghettos were radically different from the ghettos of today. The modern ghetto, Breggin observes, "is a dull and lifeless place. Much of the 'action' on the streets often consists of crimes of violence or the sale of drugs and stolen goods. The people often feel downtrodden, humiliated and hopeless. Whole families are unemployed rather than employed. There is little upward mobility and much frustration."[69]

What accounts for the marked contrast between these two different worlds? Breggin recognizes that some of the stagnation found in contemporary ghettos "results from a racist exclusion of certain groups from the mainstream of society, as well as from historic factors, such as slavery and its lingering effects." But there is no question in Breggin's mind that the greatest cause of the contrast

> is government control over the lives of the citizens in the ghetto. For example, in my own city, Washington, D.C., vendors are not allowed upon the streets without a government license, and these licenses are given out in limited numbers to those who know how to get them. As for the selling of fruits, vegetables, fish or other readily available food produced from nearby farms and waters, this is made impossible by a host of public health and business restrictions.[70]

Breggin continues by noting some of the many ways in which the State has effectively closed many of the doors to self-improvement and self-advancement used by inhabitants of earlier ghettos. Today, he notes,

> The entire ghetto family could rarely be employed because the minimum wage laws create unemployment by making it virtually impossible for small, local businessmen to profitably employ wholly unskilled youngsters. Indeed, welfare payment makes it unprofitable for many adults to work, and further encourages the stagnation. As for starting a business, it takes a genius (or a person with payoff money) to figure his way through the labyrinth of regulations and building codes.[71]

197

Breggin thinks there is an obvious lesson to be learned from all of this. The contrast between the old ghetto and the new ghetto "can demonstrate to the liberal a new starting point for helping the disadvantaged. The poor need <u>freedom</u>--freedom from government control. Freedom is what made America a haven for the poor, and freedom is what made it possible for the poor immigrant parents of the advantaged liberal to work their way into a position of advantage."72

Critics of the market who argue that capitalism obstructs the advance of freedom and justice among the poor and disadvantaged cannot find support for their claim through an appeal to the experience of American immigrants. As Breggin indicates, the unrelieved misery of those who occupy today's ghettos appears to be the responsibility of those who have by-passed the market and sought solutions through statist measures.

Whatever the reasons, it does seem clear that many of the objections to the free market are a facade that disguises the irrational character of the real objections to the system. Opposition to the market appears to be grounded more in psychological than in logical considerations. Perhaps the time has come to recognize that freedom and justice thrive best in the absence of a paternalistic statism.

NOTES

Chapter One

1. Frank S. Meyer, In Defense of Freedom (South Bend: Regnery/Gateway, 1962) p. 82.

2. Two additional points are necessary to avoid possible misunderstandings. (1) The individuals who constitute the State exercise their control through the use of many tools and instruments, e.g., laws, courts, prisons. Because of this, the term "state" is sometimes used in contexts where the institutions of the State are more in view than the individuals who use the institutions. (2) An obvious difference exists in the State between an office and the person who holds the office. A change of officeholder does not always mean a change in the State. An analogy with a professional baseball team may help to make this clear. Major league baseball teams may undergo many personnel changes in a short time. Even though the positions like first base, center field, and manager remain the same, they are often filled by different people. Yet the team retains its identity and continuity with the past. Similarly, a change in the individuals who fill the various offices of a State need not entail that the State has changed. Much depends on the prominence of the office within the hierarchy. Clearly a change of king or president will affect the identity of the State more than the replacement of a commissioner of insurance. Moreover, new officeholders may share so many convictions and values of their predecessors that few new policies result from the change.

3. Felix Morley, The Power in the People (New York: D. Van Nostrand Co., Inc., 1949) p. 106.

4. Ibid.

5. Ibid., p. 111.

6. Robert A. Nisbet, Community and Power (New York: Oxford University Press, 1962) p. 127.

7. All political philosophers recognize that in addition to their insistence on a monopoly of power within their territory, States have another feature in common. If a State were nothing more than an instrument of coercion, it would hardly differ from a highwayman or pirate who, for a time, might manage to exercise a monopoly of coercion within a particular area. States differ from robber bands by claiming a right to exist. The State's claim to legitimacy is a complex notion not within the scope of this study.

8. Quoted by Albert Jay Nock in his book, Our Enemy, The State (New York: Arno Press, 1972) p. 1. Nock does not identify the source.

9. Nock, op. cit., p. 3.

10. Morley, op. cit., p. 112.

11. The use of the numbers, 0 and 100 in the schema, has many advantages over traditional labels like "right" and "left" which, in this context, can be misleading. Anarchism and totalitarianism may be either rightist or leftist.

12. Nisbet., op. cit., pp. 145-146.

13. Ibid., p. 151.

14. The quotations come from Mussolini's comparatively short tract, The Doctrine of Fascism, that has been reprinted many times. One available source is: Benito Mussolini, Fascism, Doctrine and Institutions (New York: Howard Fertig, 1968). See especially pages 7-14.

15. The critique of political rationalism is neither an attack on reason itself nor a plea for irrationalism in politics. It is an appeal for men to recognize the proper limits of reason in the political and social order.

16. The term "mechanical" is used in contrast with "purposeful" or "teleological." The order that results from the market process is not the consequence of a human plan or design.

17. Adam Ferguson, An Essay on the History of Civil Society (London, 1967 reprint) p. 187.

18   Friedrich Hayek, _Individualism_ and _Economic Order_ (Chicago: University of Chicago Press, 1948) pp. 6-7.

19.   A non-technical discussion of the evidence for this claim can be found in _The Incredible Bread Machine_ by Susan Love Brown, et al (San Diego, California: World Research, Inc., 1974) chapter two.

20.   This apt analogy first appears, to my knowledge in the writings of Adam Smith.   As Smith described the political rationalists of his day, he (the rationalist) "seems to imagine that he can arrange the different members of a great society with as much ease as the hand arranges the different pieces upon a chessboard.   He does not consider that the pieces upon the chessboard have no other principle of motion besides that which the hand impresses upon them; but that, in the great chessboard of human society, every single piece has a principle of motion of its own, altogether different from that which the legislature might choose to impress upon it.   If those two principles coincide and act in the same direction, the game of human society will· go on easily and harmoniously, and is very likely to be happy and successful.   If they are opposite or different, the game will go on miserably and the society must be at all times in the highest degree of disorder."   Adam Smith, _Theory of Moral Sentiment_ (London: George Bell and Sons, 1907) p. 343.

21.   Nisbet, op. cit., p. 282.

22.   Ibid.

23.   Ibid., p. 283.

24.   Ibid., p. 201.

25.   Ibid., p. 202.

26.   Ibid.

27.   Ibid.

28.   Ibid., p. 283.

29.   Ibid., pp. 283-284.

30.   Ibid., p. 284.

31.   M. Stanton Evans, _Clear and Present Dangers_ (New York: Harcourt, Brace, Jovanovich, 1975) p. 34.

32.   Ibid.

33. Quoted in The Congressional Quarterly, Sept. 18, 1964.

34. In Edward Reed, ed., Challenges To Democracy (New York: Frederick A. Praeger, 1963) p. 148.

35. Harry Girvetz, The Evolution of Liberalism (New York: Collier Books, 1963) p. 65.

36. Ibid., p. 14. Additional pages where Girvetz endorses statism are pp. 250-261.

37. Senator Joseph S. Clark, "Can the Liberals Rally?", Atlantic Monthly, July, 1953.

38. Wilhelm Röpke, A Humane Economy (Indianapolis: Liberty Press, 1971) p. 33.

39. Meyer, op. cit., p. 103.

40. Ibid., p. 125.

41. Murray N. Rothbard, "The Anatomy of the State," in The Libertarian Alternative, edited by Tibor Machan (Chicago: Nelson Hall, 1974) pp. 76-77.

42. Ibid.

43. Ibid. Additional discussions of this point can be found in Bertrand De Jouvenal, On Power (New York: Viking Press, 1949) and Charles L Black, Jr., The People and the Court (New York: Macmillan, 1960).

44. For other examples, see Evans, Clear and Present Dangers, op. cit., ch. two.

45. An influential and distinctly different case for anarchism has been argued in Robert Paul Wolff's book, In Defense of Anarchism (New York: Harper and Row, 1970). A highly regarded reply to Wolff can be found in Jeffrey Reiman's In Defense of Political Philosophy (New York: Harper and Row, 1972). An interesting critique of Wolff written by a leading libertarian philosopher can be found in Tibor Machan's Human Rights and Human Liberties (Chicago: Nelson Hall, 1975) pp. 144-146.

46. Murray N. Rothbard, For a New Liberty (New York: Macmillan, 1973) p. 48.

47. Albert Jay Nock, On Doing the Right Thing, and Other Essays (New York: Harper and Bros., 1928) p. 143.

48. John Hospers, "What Libertarianism Is," The Libertarian Alternative, op. cit., p. 12.

49. Franz Oppenheimer, The State (New York: Vanguard Press, 1926) pp. 24ff.

50. Machan, Human Rights, op. cit., p. 143.

51. Ibid., p. 144.

52. Anarcho-capitalism has been expounded and defended in several books: Murray Rothbard, For a New Liberty, op. cit.; Jerome Tuccille, Radical Libertarianism (Indianapolis: Bobbs-Merrill, 1970); and David Friedman, The Machinery of Freedom (New Rochelle: Arlington House, 1978).

53. Tuccille, op. cit., p. 57.

54. Friedman, op. cit., p. 197.

55. Nozick's full argument should be consulted. See Robert Nozick, Anarchy, State and Utopia (New York: Basic Books, 1974) pp. 12ff. For an attempted answer to Nozick, see John T. Sanders, The Ethical Argument Against Government (Washington, D.C.: University Press of America, 1980) Chapter Ten.

56. M. Stanton Evans, "The Conservative Case For Freedom," Modern Age, Fall, 1960, p. 369.

57. Ibid., p. 370.

58. The Federalist, #51.

59. E.g., the power to collect taxes.

60. E.g., "No title of Nobility shall be granted by the United States," and "Congress shall make no law respecting an establishment of religion, or prohibiting the free exercise thereof."

61. The Federalist, #51.

62. Frank S. Meyer, "Conservatism," in Left, Right and Center, ed. Robert A. Goldwin (Chicago: Rand McNally and Co., 1967) p. 8.

63. Milton Friedman, Capitalism and Freedom (Chicago: University of Chicago Press, 1962) p. 34.

64. Friedrich Hayek, Law, Legislation and Liberty, vol. 3 (Chicago: University of Chicago Press, 1979) p. 41.

65. Ibid., p. 46. Friedman's well-known suggestion about public financing of privately operated educational institutions is one example of what Hayek has in mind. See Capitalism and Freedom, op. cit., Chapter VI.

Chapter Two

1. Robert Nozick, Anarchy, State and Utopia (New York: Basic Books, 1974) p. 149.
2. Friedrich Hayek, Law, Legislation and Liberty, Vol. II (Chicago: University of Chicago Press, 1976) pp. 66–67.
3. Baruch Brody, Beginning Philosophy (Englewood Cliffs, New Jersey: Prentice-Hall, 1977) p. 75.
4. Aristotle's examination of justice is found in book five of his Nichomachean Ethics.
5. See Jer. 9:24; II Sam. 23:3; Prov. 20:7; Isa. 26:7; Ps. 82:3; Micah 6:8; Job 29:14-17; II Cor. 9:8-10; and so on.
6. Richard Wollheim, "Equality," Aristotelian Society Supplement, 1956, p. 300.
7. J. Salwyn Schapiro, Liberalism: Its Meaning and History (Princeton, New Jersey: D. Van Nostrand Co., 1958) p. 10.
8. Nozick, op. cit., pp. 232f.
9. Chaim Perelman, The Idea of Justice and the Problem of Argument (New York: Humanities Press, 1963) chapter one.
10. Nicholas Rescher, Distributive Justice (New York: The Bobbs-Merrill Co., 1966) pp. 81-82.
11. George Mavrodes, "Morality, Equality and the Public Order," unpublished paper delivered at Hillsdale College, Hillsdale, Michigan, p. 5. The paper is copyrighted by the college's Center for Constructive Alternatives, 1979.
12. Ibid., p. 6.
13. William Frankena, Some Beliefs About Justice, 1966 Lindley Lecture, used by permission, Department of Philosophy, University of Kansas.

14. Nozick, op. cit., p. 154.
15. Ibid., p. 155.
16. Ibid., p. 168.
17. Ibid., pp. 149-150.
18. B. J. Diggs, "Liberty Without Fraternity," Ethics, Vol 87 (1977) p. 105.
19. In chapter seven of his book, Nozick supports this kind of reasoning with several ingenious examples that deserve careful study.

20. Nozick, op. cit., p. 163.

21. Hayek, Law, II, op. cit., p. 136.

22. Ibid., p. 67.

23. John Rawls, A Theory of Justice (Cambridge, Mass.: Harvard University Press, 1971) pp. 83-90.

24. Ibid., p. 86.

25. Ibid., p. 89.

26. Joel Feinberg, Social Philosophy (Englewood Cliffs, New Jersey: Prentice-Hall, 1973) pp. 118-119.

27. Rawls, op. cit., pp. 87-88.

28. Hayek, Law, II, op. cit., p. 87.

29. Norman Furniss and Timothy Tilton, The Case for the Welfare State (Bloomington, In.: Indiana University Press, 1977) p. 23.

30. Sidney Hook, "'Welfare State'--a Debate that Isn't," in The Welfare State, edited by E. I. Schottland (New York: Harper and Row, 1967) p. 167.

31. Furniss, op. cit.

32. Donald J. Devine, "Welfare Without Injustice," Modern Age, 1977, p. 161.

33. Ibid.

34. Ibid., p. 165.

35. M. Stanton Evans, Clear and Present Dangers (New York: Harcourt, Brace, Jovanovich, 1975).

36. Norman E. Bowie, "Welfare and Freedom," Ethics, 1979, pp. 261-2.

37. Ibid., p. 262. Further points along these lines are made by Edward Banfield in his book, The Unheavenly City (Boston: Little, Brown & Co., 1968).

38. This might be done, for example, through vouchers returned to the taxpayer. The vouchers could only be redeemed by recognized organizations.

39. Evans, op. cit., p. 127. Evans documents these claims.

40. Ibid., pp. 127-128.

41. Daniel Bell, "On Meritocracy and Equality," Public Interest, 1972, p. 72.

42. Friedrich Hayek, _Law_, II. op. cit., p. 100. Hayek's statement is one of the most puzzling he has ever written. He may have been so impressed by what he took to be Rawls' position on procedural justice that he overlooked Rawls' many statist views.

43. John Hospers, a review of _A Theory of Justice_ in _The Freeman_, December, 1973, p. 753.

44. R. M. Hare, "Rawls' Theory of Justice," _The Philosophical Quarterly_, 1973, p. 251.

45. Rawls, op. cit., p. 60.

46. The argument is adapted from Brian Barry, _The Liberal Theory of Justice_ (Oxford: Clarendon Press, 1973) pp. 16-17.

47. Hospers, _Freeman_, op. cit., p. 755.

48. Ibid.

49. Ibid.

50. Hayek, _Law_, II, op. cit., p. 66.

51. Such a stance is taken in a recent book by one of my colleagues. See Robert K. Johnston, _Evangelicals At An Impasse_ (Richmond, Va.: John Knox Press). See also "Egalitarian Aspects of the Biblical Theory of Justice" by Stephen Charles Mott in _Selected Papers of the American Society of Christian Ethics_, 1978.

52. Many of these verses were identified earlier in the chapter.

53. A common reply to this claim appeals to the Old Testament notion of a Year of Jubilee, a move effectively blunted by George Mavrodes' article, "Jubilee—A Viable Model?", _The Reformed Journal_, Jan. 1978, pp. 15-19.

54. Brody, op. cit., p. 75.

Chapter Three

1. _The Writings of Abraham Lincoln_, ed. A. B. Lapsley (New York, 1906) Vol. VII, p. 121.

2. C. L. Becker, _New Liberties For Old_ (New Haven, Conn.: Yale University Press, 1941) p. 4.

3. Edmund Burke, _Reflections on the Revolution in France_ (London, 1910) p. 6.

4. James Fitzjames Stephen, Liberty, Equality, Fraternity, 1st ed. (New York: Holt and Williams, 1873) p. 49.

5. Joel Feinberg and Hyman Gross, Liberty: Selected Readings (Encino, California: Dickenson Publishing Co., 1977) p. 4.

6. Ibid.

7. Friedrich Hayek, The Constitution of Liberty (Chicago: Henry Regnery Co., 1972) p. 16.

8. This has been argued persuasively by Gerald MacCallum, Jr., in his article, "Negative and Positive Freedom," The Philosophical Review, 1967, pp. 312-334. The examples used are drawn from MacCallum's discussion.

9. Joel Feinberg, Social Philosophy (Englewood Cliffs, New Jersey: Prentice-Hall, 1973) pp. 12f.

10. Ibid., p. 13.

11. MacCallum, op. cit.

12. An acceptance of MacCallum's triadic notion of freedom does not undercut the primacy of the absence of coercion in the analysis. It is always possible to specify what would be required for any person to be free in the negative sense; he must be free from coercion. But it is difficult, if not impossible, to specify what it would be for any person to be free in the positive sense. Our account would vary considerably for different persons in different situations. No one account of positive liberty then seems possible. As James Sterba admits, "this asymmetry between the negative and positive aspects of liberty provides at least some justification for the libertarian view that liberty functions primarily as a negative social ideal." See Sterba, "Neo-Libertarianism," American Philosophical Quarterly, Vol. 15 (1978) p. 117.

13. Section 57.

14. Murray N. Rothbard, For a New Liberty (New York: The Macmillan Co., 1973) p. 43.

15. Frank Meyer, In Defense of Freedom (South Bend: Regnery/Gateway, 1962) p. 72.

16. Robert Nozick, Anarchy, State and Utopia (New York: Basic Books, 1974) p. ix.

17. Leo Strauss, <u>Natural</u> <u>Right</u> <u>and</u> <u>History</u>
(Chicago: University of Chicago Press, 1953) p. 2.
18. L. T. Hobhouse, <u>Elements</u> <u>of</u> <u>Social</u>
Justice (London, 1922) p. 95.
19. Feinberg, <u>Social</u> <u>Philosophy</u>, op. cit.,
p. 109. Interestingly, Feinberg goes on to add an
important qualification: "Adding a right to an
equal share of the economic pie, however, is to
add a benefit of a wholly different order, one
whose presence on the list of goods for which mere
humanity is the sole qualifying condition is not
likely to win wide assent without further argument." Ibid.

Chapter Four

1. Frank S. Meyer, <u>The</u> <u>Conservative</u> <u>Main-</u>
<u>stream</u> (New York: Arlington House, 1968) pp. 76,
77.
2. Frank Meyer, <u>In</u> <u>Defense</u> <u>of</u> <u>Freedom</u>
(South Bend: Regnery/Gateway, 1962) p. 2.
3. M. Stanton Evans, "A Conservative Case
for Freedom," in <u>What</u> <u>is</u> <u>Conservatism</u>? edited by
Frank Meyer (New York: Holt, Rinehart and Winston,
1965) p. 72.
4. Frank Meyer, <u>Mainstream</u>, op. cit., p. 54.
5. Without question, the best known contemporary traditionalist is Russell Kirk. See his
<u>The</u> <u>Conservative</u> <u>Mind</u> (South Bend: Regnery/
Gateway, 1972).
6. Frank Meyer, "Freedom, Tradition, Con-
servatism" in <u>What</u> <u>is</u> <u>Conservatism</u>?, op. cit.,
p. 8.
7. Ibid., pp. 7-8. Compare also the following: "For ours is the most effective effort ever
made to articulate in <u>political</u> terms the Western
understanding of the interrelation of the freedom
of the person and the authority of an objective
moral order." Ibid., p. 8.
8. Meyer, <u>Mainstream</u>, op. cit., p. 56.
9. Ibid., p. 45.
10. Meyer, <u>Defense</u>, op. cit., p. 130.
11. Ibid., p. 145.
12. Ibid., p. 146.

13. Ibid., pp. 130-131.
14. Ibid., p. 141.
15. Sir David Ross, The Right and the Good (Oxford: The Clarendon Press, 1930).
16. See Meyer's Defense, op. cit., pp. 146ff.
17. Thomas Aquinas, Commentary on the Nicomachean Ethics, tr. by C. I. Litzinger, O.P., Vol. I, Lect. One. C.4 (South Bend: Regnery/ Gateway, 1964) p. 7.
18. Friedrich Hayek, Individualism and Economic Order (Chicago: University of Chicago Press, 1948) p. 23.
19. Ibid.
20. William Lillie, An Introduction to Ethics (New York: Barnes and Noble, 1961) p. 239.
21. Ibid.
22. Aristotle, Nichomachean Ethics, 2.1. 1103b. It should be remembered, however, that a "state" for Aristotle was a lot more like a family or a church than the modern State is. Aristotle had a relatively intimate society in mind.
23. Walter Berns, Freedom, Virtue and the First Amendment (South Bend: Regnery/Gateway, 1965) p. 253.
24. L. Brent Bozell, "Freedom or Virtue?", National Review, Sept. 11, 1962, pp. 184ff.
25. Harry M. Clor, Obscenity and Public Morality (Chicago: University of Chicago Press, 1969) p. 183.
26. Ernest Van Den Haag, "Quia Ineptum," in the book, "To Deprave and Corrupt...": Original Studies in the Nature and Definition of "Obscenity," edited by John Chandos (Chicago: Follett Publishing Co., 1962) p. 113.
27. Clor, op. cit., p. 188.
28. Ibid., pp. 188, 189.
29. Clor, op. cit., pp. 187 and 186.
30. Lord Devlin, The Enforcement of Morals (London: Oxford University Press, 1965) p. 104.
31. Ibid., p. 111.
32. Clor, op. cit., p. 188.
33. See Murray N. Rothbard, For a New Liberty (New York: The Macmillan Co., 1973) p. 106.
34. See Friedman, The Machinery of Freedom (New Rochelle: Arlington House, 1978) pp. 118ff.

35. Ibid., p. 118.

36. Ibid., p. 119.

37. William F. Buckley, Jr., The Governor Listeth (New York: G. P. Putnam's Sons, 1970) pp. 132-133.

38. Irving Kristol, "Pornography, Obscenity, and the Case for Censorship," The New York Times Magazine, March 28, 1971.

39. For more on paternalism, see Joel Feinberg, Social Philosophy (Englewood Cliffs, New Jersey: Prentice-Hall, 1973) pp. 45ff.

40. Ibid., p. 26.

41. John Stuart Mill, On Liberty (Indianapolis: Bobbs-Merrill, 1956) p. 68. Mill's book was first published in 1859.

42. Feinberg, Social Philosophy, op. cit., pp. 44-45.

43. Louis B. Schwartz, "Morals Offenses and the Model Penal Code," Columbia Law Review, Volume 63 (1963) p. 669.

44. "Report of the Committee on Homosexual Offenses and Prostitution Presented to Parliament by the Secretary of State for the Home Department and the Secretary of State for Scotland by Command of Her Majesty," September 1957 (Cmmd. 247) para. 13.

45. Devlin, op. cit.

46. See the discussion of this and related points earlier in this chapter. Devlin seems to have held both the second and third theories about the relationship between morality and society.

47. See H. L. A. Hart, Law, Liberty and Morality (Stanford, California: Stanford University Press, 1963).

48. Bruce Kaye and Gordon Wenham, Law, Morality and the Bible (Downers Grove, Illinois: Intervarsity Press, 1978) p. 239.

Chapter Five

1. Wilhelm Röpke, Economics of the Free Society (Chicago: Henry Regnery Co., 1960) p. 259.

2. Ludwig Von Mises, Human Action (New Haven, Conn.: Yale University Press, 1949) pp. 257-258.

3. This point is discussed in more detail in the next chapter. For more on the State's indispensable role in monopoly, see Yale Brozen, "Is Government the Source of Monopoly?", The Intercollegiate Review, Volume 5, Winter 1968-69, pp. 67-78; and Milton Friedman, Capitalism and Freedom (Chicago: University of Chicago Press, 1962) chapter VIII.

4. John Hospers, "Free Enterprise as the Embodiment of Justice," in Ethics, Free Enterprise and Public Policy, edited by Richard T. DeGeorge and Joseph A. Picheler (New York: Oxford University Press, 1978) p. 71.

5. See Friedman, op. cit., chapter IX.

6. A non-technical but still competent defense of this claim can be found in The Incredible Bread Machine by Susan Love Brown, et al. (San Diego: World Research, Inc., 1974) chapters one and two.

7. Friedrich Hayek, The Constitution of Liberty (Chicago: Henry Regnery Co., 1972) p. 220.

8. Henry Hazlitt, The Foundations of Morality (New York: Van Nostrand, 1964) p. 326.

9. Interesting admission along this line can be found in The Capitalist System, edited by Richard C. Edwards, Michael Reich, and Thomas E. Weiskopf (Englewood Cliffs, New Jersey: Prentice-Hall, 2nd edition, 1978). See pages xii and 532.

10. Michael Lerner, The New Socialist Revolution: An Introduction to Its Theory and Strategy (New York: Delacorte Press, 1973), cited in Edwards, op. cit., p. 538.

11. Serge Mallet, "Bureaucracy and Technology in the Socialist Countries," Socialist Revolution, 1, No. 3 (May/June 1970) p. 45.

12. Lerner, op. cit., p. 532.

13. David Ramsay Steele, "Lange's Theory of Socialism After Forty Years," Austrian Economics Newsletter, 1978, Vol. I, 3, p. 4. Steele documents the non-market nature of socialist theories during the first two decades of the twentieth century.

14. See Lancelot Lawton, Economic History of Soviet Russia (London, 1922) and Paul Craig Roberts, Alienation and the Soviet Economy (Albuguerque: University of New Mexico Press, 1971).

15. Steele, op. cit., p. 12. Steele's entire critique should be read. He carefully unmasks fundamental equivocations in the views Lange set forth over the years that make it difficult to believe that many who cite Lange's works have ever read them. For those who would like to read Lange for the first time, the reference is Oscar Lange and Fred Taylor, On the Economic Theory of Socialism (New York: McGraw-Hill, 1938).

16. Henry Hazlitt, Foundations, op. cit., p. 304.

17. Ibid. For general discussions of attempts to refute Mises, see T. J. B. Hoff, Economic Calculation in the Socialist Society (London: Hodge, 1949); Friedrich Hayek, Individualism and Economic Order (Chicago: University of Chicago Press, 1948); and Roberts, Alienation and the Soviet Economy, op. cit. Also worth consulting is Murray N. Rothbard, "Ludwig Von Mises and Economic Calculation Under Socialism," in The Economics of Ludwig Von Mises, ed. Laurence S. Moss (Kansas City: Sheed and Ward, 1976) pp. 67-78.

18. Ludwig Von Mises, Socialism (New Haven: Yale University Press, 1951) p. 122.

19. Ludwig Von Mises, Human Action (Chicago: Contemporary Books, Third Revised Edition, 1966) p. 706.

20. The Road to Serfdom (Chicago: University of Chicago Press, 1944).

21. Herbert Marcuse, An Essay On Liberation (Boston: Beacon Press, 1969) p. 11.

22. Ibid., pp. xiii-xiv.

23. Ibid., pp. 24-25.

24. Herbert Marcuse, One-Dimensional Man (Boston: Beacon Press, 1964) chapter one. Later quotations from Marcuse's essay in A Critique of Pure Tolerance make it clear that his revulsion at dictatorial tribunals was short-lived, at

least in the case of tribunals that included him
as a member.

25. Described in one of three essays in the
book, A Critique of Pure Tolerance by Marcuse,
R. P. Wolff and Barrington Moore, Jr. (Boston:
Beacon Press, 1967).

26. Marcuse, Critique, op. cit., p. 109.

27. "For the true positive is the society of
the future and therefore beyond definition and
and determination, while the existing positive is
that which must be surmounted." Ibid., p. 87.

28. Dale Vree, a former student radical and
Marxist agitator during the campus unrest in the
1960's, acknowledges the duplicity of Marxist
endorsements of liberty. He writes, "As a Marxist-
Leninist, I was quite aware that post-capitalist
society would be characterized by dictatorship,
secret police, censorship, a command economy, and
the like. Indeed, I characterized myself as
something of a 'neo-Stalinist'.... I was quite
aware of the harsh, 'agressive' measures that
would have to be taken in order to reach communism. I would go so far as to say that I consciously practiced verbal deception when propagan-
dizing for the communist cause--that is, I would
condemn capitalism for being insufficiently
'affectional,' insufficiently libertarian, all the
while recognizing that a socialist dictatorship
would be far less 'affectional,' far less libertarian, than the capitalism I was condemning."
Dale Vree, "A Comment on 'Some Irrational Sources
of Opposition to the Market System,'" in
Capitalism: Sources of Hostility, edited by
Ernest van den Haag (New Rochelle, Epoch Books,
1979) pp. 155-156.

29. Essay on Liberation, op. cit., p. xiv.

30. It is little wonder that at one stage of
his thought Marcuse wondered wistfully if "perhaps an accident [might] alter the situation..."
But as he continued, "Unless the recognition of
what is being done and what is being prevented
subverts the consciousness and the behavior of
man, not even a catastrophe will bring about the
change." Essay on Liberation, op. cit., p. xv.

31. Ludwig Von Mises, A Critique of Interventionism, tr. by Hans Sennholz (New Rochelle,
New York: Arlington House, 1977) p. 151.
32. Time, October 10, 1969, p. 94.
33. See Warren L. Coats, Jr., "The Economics
of Discrimination," Modern Age, 1974, p. 68.
34. Murray N. Rothbard, America's Great
Depression (Kansas City, Kansas: Sheed and Ward,
1975) from the Introduction to the Third Edition,
no pagination. See also Lawrence W. Reed, "The
Silver Panic," The Freeman, June, 1978, pp. 366-
377.
35. Henry Hazlitt, "Inflation in One Page,"
The Freeman, May, 1978, p. 276f.
36. Ibid., p. 277. George Reisman provides
extensive documentation for these claims in his
book, The Government Against the Economy (Ottawa,
Illinois: Caroline House Publishers, Inc., 1979).
37. Rothbard, Depression, op. cit., Introduction to Third Edition.

Chapter Six

1. Irving Kristol, "A Capitalist Conception
of Justice," in Ethics, Free Enterprise and Public
Policy, edited by Richard T. DeGeorge and
Joseph A. Pichler (New York: Oxford University
Press, 1978) p. 57.
2. Israel Kirzner, "The Ugly Market: Why
Capitalism is Hated, Feared and Despised," The
Freeman, Dec., 1974, pp. 724-5. Kirzner's article
is an excellent summary of several fallacies com-
mited by critics of the market.
3. F. A. Hayek, editor, Capitalism and the
Historians (Chicago: University of Chicago Press,
1954) pp. 9-10.
4. Bertrand Russell, The Impact of Science
on Society (New York: Columbia University Press,
1951) pp. 19-20.
Susan Love Brown, et al., The Incredible
Bread Machine (San Diego, California: World
Research, Inc., 1974) p. 25.
6. Ibid., pp. 25-26.

7.   Henry Hazlitt, The Foundations of Morality (Van Nostrand, 1964) p. 325.

8.   Robert Nozick, Anarchy, State and Utopia (New York: Basic Books, 1974) pp. 253-262.

9.   Ibid., p. 255.

10.   Ibid.

11.   Ibid., pp. 255-256.

12.   Ibid., p. 256.

13.   Ibid.

14.   Richard T. DeGeorge, "Moral Issues in Business," in Ethics, Free Enterprise and Public Policy, op. cit., p. 11.

15.   William Coates, God in Public (Grand Rapids: Eerdmans Publishing Co., 1974) p. 184.

16.   Tom Christoffel, David Finkelhor and Dan Gilbarg, editors, Up Against The American Myth (New York: Holt, Rinehart and Winston, 1970) p. 15.

17.   Murray N. Rothbard, Power and Market (Kansas City: Sheed Andrews and McMeel, Inc., 2nd edition, 1977) p. 208.

18.   Henry Hazlitt, "Planning vs. the Free Market," Essays in Liberty (Irvington-on-Hudson, New York: The Foundation for Economic Education, 1963) volume X, pp. 183-184.

19.   Rothbard, Power, op. cit. Several aspects of this problem have already been covered in earlier discussion of Marcuse.

20.   Ibid.

21.   Ludwig Von Mises, "On Equality and Inequality," Modern Age, 1961, p. 142.

22.   Israel Kirzner, "Equilibrium versus Market Process," in The Foundations of Austrian Economics, ed. Edwin G. Dolan (Kansas City, Kansas: Sheed and Ward, Inc., 1976) p. 121.

23.   Ibid., p. 122.

24.   Ibid., p. 123.

25.   All of these questions about advertising are addressed with competence in the book, Advertising and Society, ed. Yale Brozen (New York: New York University Press, 1974).

26.   See Brozen, op. cit., p. 84.

27.   Harold Demsetz, "Advertising in the Affluent Society," in Brozen, op. cit., p. 70.

28. Philip J. Nelson, "The Economic Value of Advertising," ibid., p. 64.

29. John Arthur and William H. Shaw, Justice and Economic Distribution (Englewood Cliffs, New Jersey: Prentice-Hall, 1978) p. 180.

30. Norman E. Bowie and Robert L. Simon, The Individual and the Political Order (Englewood Cliffs, New Jersey: Prentice-Hall, 1977) p. 195.

31. Milton Friedman, Capitalism and Freedom (Chicago: University of Chicago Press, 1962) pp. 27-28. Most of Friedman's book is relevant to this problem.

32. Ibid., p. 30.

33. See Friedman, op. cit., chapter VI.

34. David Friedman, The Machinery of Freedom (New Rochelle: Arlington House, 1978) p. 139.

35. Ibid., pp. 140-141.

36. These manuscripts along with a helpful introduction can be found in Karl Marx, Early Writings, translated and edited by T. B. Bottomore (New York: McGraw-Hill Book Co., 1964).

37. DeGeorge, op. cit., p. 12.

38. Ibid.

39. Paul Sweezy, "Socialism and Communism as Ideals," Monthly Review, 1963, reprinted in Up Against The American Myth, op. cit., p. 417.

40. Murray N. Rothbard, America's Great Depression (Kansas City: Sheed and Ward, 1975) p. 2.

41. Ibid.

42. Ibid., p. 3.

43. Henry Hazlitt, "Gold Versus Fractional Reserves," The Freeman, 1979, p. 264.

44. Ibid., pp. 264-265.

45. Bread Machine, op. cit., pp. 32, 33.

46. Rothbard, Power and Market, op. cit., p. 205.

47. Ibid.

48. Donald Devine, Does Freedom Work? (Ottawa, Illinois: Caroline House Books, 1978) p. 44.

49. Kirzner, "Equilibrium," op. cit., p. 116.

50. Ibid.

51. Devine, op. cit., p. 52.

52. Ibid.

53. Ibid., pp. 52-53. See Devine's book for statistical support for his claims. See also Yale Brozen, "The Antitrust Task Force Deconcentration Recommendation," Journal of Law and Economics, 1970, pp. 279-292.

54. See Friedman, Capitalism and Freedom, op. cit., chapters VIII-IX.

55. William L. Baker, "Marx and the Manifesto," The Freeman, 1979, pp. 681-2.

56. Ibid., p. 683.

57. The view that economic value is subjective does not entail the subjectivity of other types of value such as moral value.

58. Arthur, Justice, op. cit., p. 181.

59. Bowie, The Individual, op. cit., p. 194.

60. Rothbard, Power and Market, op. cit., p. 205.

61. Ernest Van Den Haag, Capitalism: Sources of Hostility (New Rochelle, New York: Epoch Books, 1979) p. 11.

62. Ibid., p. 12.

63. Kirzner, "The Ugly Market," op. cit., p. 733. Robert Nozick includes an excellent discussion of the role envy plays in opposition to the market. See his Anarchy, State and Utopia, op. cit., chapter 8.

64. James Burnham, Suicide of the West (New York: John Day, 1964).

65. Peter R. Breggin, "Libertarianism and the Liberal Ethos," The Libertarian Review, November, 1979 (vol. 8) p. 31.

66. Ibid.

67. Ibid., p. 32.

68. Ibid., p. 34.

69. Ibid.

70. Ibid.

71. Ibid.

72. Ibid.

FOR FURTHER READING

Arthur, John and Shaw, William H., editors.
Justice and Economic Distribution (Englewood
Cliffs, New Jersey: Prentice-Hall, 1978).

Barry, Brian. The Liberal Theory of Justice (New
York: Oxford University Press, 1973).

Bedau, Hugo, editor. Justice and Equality (Englewood Cliffs, New Jersey: Prentice-Hall,
1971).

Berlin, Isaiah. Four Essays On Liberty (New York:
Oxford University Press, 1969).

Bowie, Norman E. and Simon, Robert L., editors.
The Individual and the Political Order
(Englewood Cliffs, New Jersey: Prentice-Hall,
1977).

Bowie, Norman E., "Welfare and Freedom," Ethics,
Vol. 89 (1979).

Brown, Susan Love, et al. The Incredible Bread
Machine (San Diego: World Research Inc.,
1974).

Brozen, Yale, "Is Government the Source of Monopoly?", The Intercollegiate Review, Vol. 5
(1968-69).

Clor, Harry M. Obscenity and Public Morality
(Chicago: University of Chicago Press, 1969).

DeGeorge, Richard T. and Picheler, Joseph A.,
editors. Ethics, Free Enterprise and Public
Policy (New York: Oxford University Press,
1978).

219

Devlin, Lord Patrick. The Enforcement of Morals
(London: Oxford University Press, 1965).

Evans, M. Stanton. Clear and Present Dangers (New
York: Harcourt Brace Jovanovich, 1975).

Feinberg, Joel and Gross, Hyman, editors. Justice:
Selected Readings (Encino, California:
Dickenson Publishing Co., 1977).

Feinberg, Joel "Legal Moralism and Freefloating
Evils," Pacific Philosophical Quarterly,
Vol. 61 (1980).

Feinberg, Joel and Gross, Hyman, editors. Liberty: Selected Readings (Encino, California:
Dickenson Publishing Co., 1977).

Feinberg, Joel. Social Philosophy (Englewood
Cliffs, New Jersey: Prentice-Hall, 1973).

Friedman, David. The Machinery of Freedom (New
Rochelle: Arlington House, 1978).

Friedman, Milton. Capitalism and Freedom (Chicago:
University of Chicago Press, 1962).

Friedrich, C. J. and Chapman, J., editors.
Justice (New York: Aldine-Atherton, 1963).

Friedrich, Carl J., editor. Liberty (New York:
Atherton Press, 1962).

Hacker, P. M. S. and Raz, J. Law, Morality and
Society (New York: Oxford University Press,
1977).

Hampshire, Stuart, editor. Public and Private
Morality (New York: Cambridge University
Press, 1978).

Hart, H. L. A. Law, Liberty and Morality (New
York: Random House, 1966).

Hayek, Friedrich, editor. Capitalism and the
     Historians (Chicago: University of Chicago
     Press, 1954).

Hayek, Friedrich. The Constitution of Liberty
     (Chicago: University of Chicago Press, 1960).

Hayek, Friedrich. Law, Legislation and Liberty,
     3 volumes (Chicago: University of Chicago
     Press, 1973-1979).

Hayek, Friedrich. The Road to Serfdom (Chicago:
     University of Chicago Press, 1944).

Hospers, John. Libertarianism (Los Angeles: Nash
     Publishing Co., 1971).

Kaye, Bruce and Wenham, Gordon. Law, Morality
     and the Bible (Downers Grove, Illinois:
     Intervarsity Press, 1978).

Kelbley, Charles A. The Value of Justice (New
     York: Fordham University Press, 1979).

Kirzner, Israel. "The Ugly Market: Why Capitalism
     is Hated, Feared and Despised." The Freeman.
     Volume 24 (1974).

Leiser, Burton M. Liberty, Justice and Morals
     (New York: Macmillan, 2nd edition, 1979).

Leoni, Bruno. Freedom and the Law (New York:
     D. Van Nostrand, 1961).

MacCallum, Gerald C., Jr. "Negative and Positive
     Freedom." The Philosophical Review.
     Volume LXXVI (1967).

Machan, Tibor, editor. The Libertarain Alterna-
     tive (Chicago: Nelson-Hall, 1974).

McLean, George F. Freedom, Proceedings of the
     American Catholic Philosophical Association,
     Vol. 50 (Washington, D. C., Catholic Univer-
     sity of America, 1976).

Meyer, Frank S. In Defense of Reason (Chicago:
     Henry Regnery Co., 1962).

Mill, John Stuart. On Liberty (first published in
     1859; many editions available).

Mitchell, Basil. Law, Morality and Religion (New
     York: Oxford University Press, 1967).

Nash, Ronald H. "A Note on Marcuse and 'Libera-
     tion'." The Intercollegiate Review.
     Volume 14 (1978).

Nash, Ronald H. "The Economics of Justice."
     Christianity Today. Volume XXIII (March 23,
     1979).

Nash, Ronald H. "Three Kinds of Individualism."
     The Intercollegiate Review. Volume 12 (1976).

Nisbet, Robert. Community and Power (New York:
     Oxford University Press, 1962).

Nock, Albert Jay. Our Enemy, The State (New York:
     Arno Press, 1972).

Nozick, Robert. Anarchy, State and Utopia (New
     York: Basic Books, 1974).

Oppenheimer, Franz. The State (New York:
     Vanguard Press, 1926).

Parrent, William A. "Some Recent Work on the
     Concept of Liberty." American Philosophical
     Quarterly. Volume 11 (1974).

Perelman, Chaim. Justice (New York: Random
     House, 1967.

Rawls, John. A Theory of Justice (Cambridge,
     Massachusetts: Harvard University Press,
     1971).

Reisman, George. The Government Against the
    Economy (Ottawa, Illinois: Caroline House
    Publishers, 1979).

Röpke, Wilhelm. A Humane Economy (Chicago:
    Henry Regnery Co., 1960).

Rothbard, Murray N. America's Great Depression
    (Kansas City: Sheed and Ward, 1975).

Rothbard, Murray N. For a New Liberty (New York:
    Macmillan, 1978 revised edition).

Sanders, John T. The Ethical Argument Against
    Government (Washington, D.C.: University
    Press of America, 1980).

Schaeffer, David Lewis. Justice or Tyranny?
    A Critique of John Rawls' Theory of Justice
    (Port Washington, N.Y.: Kennikat Press,
    1979).

Schaeffer, David Lewis, editor. The New Egali-
    tarians (Port Washington, N.Y.: Kennikat
    Press, 1979.

Templeton, Kenneth S., editor. The Politicization
    of Society (Indianapolis: Liberty Press,
    1979).

Van Den Haag, Ernest, editor. Capitalism: Sources
    of Hostility (New Rochelle, New York: Epoch
    Books, 1979).

Ward, Benjamin. The Ideal Worlds of Economics
    (New York: Basic Books, 1979).

Wasserstrom, Richard, editor. Morality and the
    Law (Belmont, California: Wadsworth, 1971).

INDEX

226

Natural rights 91ff.
Need 42-43
Nelson, Philip 175
Nisbet, Robert 4, 9-12, 103ff.
Nock, Albert Jay 3
Nozick, Robert 26, 32, 35ff., 39, 46ff., 68-69,
    90, 164-165, 204

Offense 117ff., 123
Oppenheimer, Franz 21-22
Ortega y Gasset, J. 3

Paine, Thomas 95
Paternalism 113, 117ff., 123, 124
Perelman, Chaim 40
Political rationalism 5ff., 201
Pollution 178ff.
Positive rights 91ff.
Private-Harm principle 117ff.
Public-Harm principle 117ff., 123
Puritanical argument 170ff.

Quadripartite Bureaucracy 16ff.

Rawls, John 53ff., 68ff.
Rescher, Nicholas 41
Reuther, Walter 13
Rights, human 20f., 26, 27, 90ff., 95, 131
Röpke, Wilhelm 16
Ross, Sir David 105-106
Rothbard, Murray 18-19, 24, 26, 27, 90, 102, 115,
    150-153, 170, 171, 182, 185, 186, 191, 193
Rousseau, Jean Jacques 4, 69
Rule of Law 57, 88ff., 132-133
Russell, Bertrand 159

Schapiro, J. S. 38
Schwartz, Louis 121
Shaw, William 176, 191
Simon, Robert 176, 191
Smith, Adam 201

ABOUT THE AUTHOR

Ronald H. Nash is Professor of Philosophy and Head of the Department of Philosophy and Religion at Western Kentucky University, Bowling Green, Kentucky. Prior to going to Western in 1964, Nash taught at Syracuse University, Houghton College and Barrington College. After graduating from Barrington College in 1958, Nash went on to do graduate work in philosophy at Brown University and Syracuse University where he earned his M.A. and Ph.D. degrees. He has done post-doctoral study at Stanford University under a grant from the National Endowment for the Humanities. Nash's six previous books include Ideas of History (E. P. Dutton) and The Light of the Mind: St. Augustine's Theory of Knowledge (University of Kentucky Press). He has published more than twenty articles in such journals as The Intercollegiate Review, The New Scholasticism, Christian Scholars Review, Christianity Today, Augustinian Studies, Westminster Theological Journal, and The Reformed Journal.

231